UNLEASH

THE

PITCHER

IN

YOU

HECTOR L. BERRIOS

Copyright

TABLE OF CONTENTS

FOREWORD

As a professional baseball executive with over 30 years of experience in Major League Baseball, I am pleased and honored to write the foreword to *Unleash the Pitcher in You.* Although the schedule was tight, I undertook the challenge to make my humble contribution to this impressive project.

I would like to warmly congratulate the author of *Unleash the Pitcher in You,* Hector Berrios, on his initiative in bringing this book to life. He has spent a lifetime of not only teaching these methods but spending countless hours learning the proper techniques to correct pitching flaws within the delivery for quality execution.

I first met Hector in the summer of 1985, playing Minor League Baseball for the Kansas City Royals in Eugene, Oregon. This season would be the only season in which we played on the same team although our paths were destined to cross in future endeavors. Hector was an unbelievable student of the game. He was always searching for information on the opposition or hitters in general and tinkering with his pitches to give him an edge over his competition. Hector was exact on the mound; his mindset was to stay two pitches ahead of the hitter's thought process. Our conversations on bus rides and in the locker rooms were always about the game and getting better. Hector reminded me of myself minus being the "Salsa Dance instructor" for the winter employment.

The game of baseball has so many facets, and intricate areas of expertise that make *Unleash the Pitcher in You* required reading. Hector provides an intimate look from the pitching side with unmatched details and photos for a parent, coach, pitcher, or player to follow.

I played professionally, scouted players around the world, and have played a fundamental part in opening academies in Latin America with the intent of helping players develop. Additionally, I have been fortunate enough to be the VP of Player Development for the Los Angeles Dodgers, and Sr. VP of Baseball Operations for the Arizona Diamondbacks.

During my time as the VP of Player Development for the Los Angeles Dodgers, I was responsible for not only developing players but finding and growing the best instructors in the game as well. For the Major League level to achieve sustained success, the Minor League system must produce Major League talent that is ready to compete, have an impact on the game, and directly contribute to the team. That talent needs to be of championship caliber.

When we began building out our coaching staff, I researched all 30 Major League and Minor League teams, as well as college programs in search of the best teachers. The goal was to find innovative teachers/instructors with a strong desire to maximize every player on the roster. Hector's reputation for impacting young pitchers' development was extremely imposing. His vocal energy and the ability to so effortlessly converse in English and Spanish separated him from some of the other candidates.

Before requesting permission to speak with Hector about a possible employment opportunity with the Dodgers, I heard that he had completed an extensive study on pitching to the count and the scoreboard. This research made him a prime candidate that I knew was ready for the next challenge baseball had to offer him. Hector's primary roles as a professional pitching coach had been to take the 12 to 15 pitchers and help them improve.

After the interview process, I saw Hector through a different lens and felt that he needed to share his extensive knowledge and information to the masses at the entry level. The only challenge with my plan was Hector's limited exposure to teaching in this type of setting. So, I decided to put him in front of our Instructional League staff and pitchers and walk them through the importance of understanding why they should follow his methodology. It's one thing to understand the philosophy, but it is entirely different from executing a quality pitch in a quality location. For the record, Hector was a natural in front of a large audience.

Unleash the Pitcher in You has content and knowledge that leads the reader through the core concepts of pitching, which includes the delivery, the proper use of the lower half of the body and the effect of the kinetic chain link that removes stress from the arm. *Unleash the Pitcher in You* also covers the mental aspect of the game from a pitcher's perspective, challenges faced by pitchers and position players, and it provides you with the blueprint on how to identify a hitter's weakness to execute and deliver the right pitch. Hector gives you step by step physical preparation tips not only for the season but offseason as you set goals for your upcoming personal victories

Unleash the Pitcher in You is a comprehensive, in-depth compilation of experience and extensive knowledge with an emphasis on a winning pitching philosophy. It covers every facet of a pitcher, and it tackles many misconceptions and pitfalls inexperienced pitchers face throughout middle school, high school, or college baseball tryouts and games. The numerous well-documented antidotes and stories ensure that the reader will have a clear understanding of all phases of a successful pitcher.

It is evident that Hector put his heart and soul into preparing the most detailed book to get young baseball pitchers mentally and physically prepared for success. His baseball journey to get to this point helped shaped his core principles. *Unleash the Pitcher in You* contains PROFESSIONAL INSIDER INFORMATION that you won't learn at your weekly pitching lesson or summer baseball camp.

From the beginning of a lifelong friendship and throughout our dual pursuit of excellence in a game of failure, Hector has undoubtedly improved the chances for success in *Unleash the Pitcher in You.*

De Jon Watson
Washington Nationals
Special Assistant to the President and General Manager, Baseball Operations

Acknowledgments

As I begin thanking the people that have inspired me to write this book, I want to start by giving God, my heavenly father the glory. I asked him for guidance and wisdom in putting my coaching experience, through words, down on paper. The birthing of this book came when I was in a very dark and cloudy phase of my career and personal life. It was difficult not knowing where the journey of life was leading me. Being a born-again Christian, I put my faith in God, and he shined his light on me, keeping everything bright and illuminated while my thoughts poured into writing this book, and used it as a vessel to help aspiring pitchers.

I want to thank my wife Kamila Khalilova for always encouraging me to go full steam ahead with this book. It has been a long time coming since the initial time that I embarked on this quest to teach the world what I had learned as a pitching coach. She has been my biggest supporter. God has blessed me with a very resilient, intelligent, resourceful, no-nonsense, outside the box thinker, get things done type of woman. It has been an absolute blessing sharing my life with you, and I thank you for being my driving force behind the scenes.

To my three daughters, Jennifer, Jessica, and Isabella for having to be without me for months at a time, but on the other hand, I was blessed to be close to home for most of my coaching career. Working in Hagerstown, Maryland and Brooklyn, New York, I was able to be with you guys regularly. We traveled together and saw beautiful places, and for that I'm grateful. I am proud of each of you as you've grown up to be a great woman of the future and I can't wait to see what lies ahead as you keep displaying your talents to the world. I thank you for always supporting me.

God allows angels to come into our lives, to protect, teach, guide, and mature us. I want to bring to light the angels who I feel were God's blessing in writing this book. I want to thank Doris Diaz who was one of the best inspiring coaches I've ever had. She was there in my initial stages when I didn't believe I was able to write my thoughts down on paper. She motivated me to write, day in and day out, and writing I did, as I was turning in chapter after chapter on a daily and weekly basis. Once I finished a chapter, I could hear her words telling me, "come on, come on, keep writing." Doris, I will never forget your wisdom, intelligence, writing abilities and most of all, your friendship.

Razor Shines, I thank you, first and foremost, for your friendship. I had a great summer with you during the 2012 season in Midland, Michigan. We had a manager that came to me before our first game of the season and told me that I would run the pitching staff. I was responsible for who to get ready and when they would come in the game; the only thing he would do was the actual pitching change. It was the first time I had that responsibility, and that's where Razor comes into the picture. Razor had been manager of the year at several stops and had also coached at the big-league level, not to mentioned he was a former catcher himself. I went over to Razor and told him about my responsibility and that he was required to be by my side and tell me anything and everything that came to his mind when it came to pitching decisions and strategy. I learned more about running a pitching staff that summer than any other season. Razor sparked my intention to write the Cat and Mouse chapter in *Unleash the Pitcher in You*. Razor would yell at the catcher that the batter was in Swing Mode, meaning the pitcher could throw him an off-speed pitch and he would swing and miss or be out in front due to the hitter being geared up for the fastball which happened time and time again during that season. Razor, I thank you from the bottom of my heart, it was a life changing experience.

Pat Borders is one of the best and nicest human beings I have had the pleasure of spending not one, but three seasons in the dugout with him. Pat has an innate ability as well as an intuition what the hitter is thinking, feeling, and is about to do before he does it. He has an incredible gift to throw a hitter's timing off so bad, that hitters would go back to the dugout shaking their heads and talking to themselves. I had a lot of experience on setting hitters up and freezing them inside with fastballs as a pitching coach and Pat started to ask me questions about what I was doing, and it opened a relationship of a brotherly bond that has made us family. Pat Borders was a World Series MVP, he was a two-time World Series Champion and played in the Major Leagues as a catcher for 17 years. I have learned so much from Pat, that he inspired me to write The Art of Throwing Off Hitter's Timing. I thank you, Pat, for all you've taught me as well as giving me the gift of friendship.

DeJon Watson thank you for giving me the opportunity to work for the Dodgers Organization. You were there pushing me to get up on stage to do my presentation in front of the whole organization as well as the Dodger greats. Presenting in front of such a large group was nerve-racking, but today I'm as cool as a cucumber in part because of you. It allowed me to work alongside Rafael Chavez who I've learned from immensely. I remember showing you my notes on the Cat and Mouse chapter, and you always challenged me to think outside the box. You and I played together in the Kansas City organization, and there was an instant connection, which I'm proud to say we have until this very day. Thank you for being such a great teammate, boss, and most of all my eternal friend.

Rafael Chaves has been the most influential pitching coordinator I've ever worked for, and I can say it was not work. It was fun and challenging. He was always striking thoughts to make you go hmm, I didn't see it from that point of view. He allowed his pitching coaches to work with freedom, yet under the guidelines. He's been there through good times as well as the tough ones. Rafael has had one of the best runs over the last five years in Minor League Baseball having an organizational ERA and least number of walks in the top five or better of the 30 teams. Rafael and I competed in the Minor Leagues as well as in Puerto Rican Winter League, but I didn't get to know him until we worked together with the Dodgers where he was the pitching coordinator. I started to hear him talk about the lower half and hand separation. How the glove hand would naturally stay inside the front knee longer were frequent topics of conversation with all our coaches. I was so intrigued because I had a whole different school of thought. I had been around great coaches, but not until I was blessed to meet Rafael Chaves, was I able to see the pitching delivery from a whole new perspective. Since learning this delivery of the baseball, I have seen more strikes, more velocity increases, and more meteorites to the big leagues than I have ever seen in my coaching experience. The Delivery section of *Unleash the Pitcher in You* is a section that has Rafael's influence on it. I thank you, Rafael, for trusting in me as one of your coaches, your patience, your teaching and most of all your friendship is something that will stay with me for a lifetime.

I want to thank the pitchers that have made this book possible and for trusting in me and allowing me to enhance your abilities. Ronald Bolaños and Vladimir Gutiérrez are in the pictures used for the description of each movement, drill or phase of the pitching action. Ronald Bolaños was an International free agent who defected from Cuba and I was asked to work with him down in the Dominican Republic. Ronald was a former position player with little to no pitching experience when I started working with him. We worked every day for four months as he eventually landed a multimillion-dollar bonus to be a professional pitcher. Vladimir Gutiérrez also defected from Cuba and was in the United States for over nine months without getting any offers. His velocity was down and mechanics out of whack. I was asked to work with Vladimir and in little time he was up to 96 and 97mph touching 98 and it wasn't long before he was rewarded with a multimillion-dollar bonus just like Bolaños. Jacob Waguespack was an undrafted free agent who has beat the odds and is presently on a big league 40-man roster. To all the pitchers that I have worked with over my 22 years in coaching, thank you and know that I have learned how to be a better pitching coach because of the hours, days, weeks, months and in some cases years we bonded and did everything possible to make each one of you better.

I want to thank Bruce Peditto for helping and collaborating with me on the Strength and Conditioning chapter. Bruce is a true professional. He pays close attention to detail is always engaged, and the players gravitated to him. He was still very intrigued by what we did in our bullpen sessions, that we spent hours of quality time together sharing information back and forth. I couldn't have found a better person to collaborate in this section of the book, than Bruce Peditto. Bruce, I thank you for taking time out of your busy schedule to help me out on this chapter in *Unleash the Pitcher in You*. I will be eternally grateful for your knowledge, wisdom, and expertise that has resulted in you stamping your fingerprints on the Strength and Conditioning chapter.

I want to thank a person who was God sent through my daughter Jessica Berrios. She introduced me to this talented graphic design artist who was everything, if not more than he was advertised. He was able to take my vision and bring it to life on the front and back covers of the book. He always suggested his ideas but never pressured, resulting in two good teammates working jointly to get these intricate covers done. Jonathon Desrosiers, I sincerely thank you for your time, patience, creativity, and most importantly, your talent as a graphic design artist to make my dream come to life. I appreciate your friendship during this process, and we have a lot more to accomplish together on our journeys.

To bring this project to full completion, I needed a person I trusted and had the faith in knowing that they saw things from different lenses other than mine. I got in touch with Dustin Sleet to give his stamp of approval and make sure everything was close to perfection as possible. I have worked with Dustin for the last two years and he has always gone above and beyond in everything that was asked of him in a timely fashion. His attention to detail and the work he has produced is second to none. As soon as I thought everything was completed I reached out to him to clean up any mistakes and he did not let me down. I am grateful to have met you and have developed an amazing amount of trust in your work. I am honored to have you be a part of this book.

Lastly, I want to thank Sandy Daronco, the mother of one of my students Richard Daronco. One day before one of our lessons, I mentioned to her that I had written a book on pitching and she asked me to get it copyrighted so she could read it. I did just that, and she began to read it, and she became my book editor. Sandy is a former journalist with WNBC-TV and WCBS-TV in New York, and she has inspired me to incorporate pictures and meet deadlines ever since we started collaborating on *Unleash the Pitcher in You*. I can't believe how much we've gotten done in a short period. Sandy, you have been one of my all-time best teammates, and I thank you.

MISSION STATEMENT

We want to welcome you on this instructional pitching journey that will allow you to reach your highest potential. We have designed a blueprint that has a system in which if applied in detail will give you the answers and the developmental platform to enhance and master all areas of your pitching ability. When embarking on this or any program, we must have 100% commitment and dedication for you to reach your highest potential.

Attention to detail is a vital attribute to maximize your talents and gifts. It has taken over 30 years in professional baseball experience to come up with this concept that has allowed many professional pitchers to live out their childhood dreams to play in the Big Leagues. It is because of this achieved success that we are excited and confident this is the best program for you.

The focus is to teach pitchers the secrets to keeping their arms healthy for all the years they pitch in this game; as well as learning the best and most effective way to stay in optimum physical shape to come out on top of your competitors. This instructional system is for the serious athlete focused on being the best they can be. It is a fact that if we are committed, determined, passionate, willing to persevere, and not take no for an answer, the chances of succeeding are far higher.

Unleash The Pitcher In You is a comprehensive approach, to developing a pitcher from the ground up--from the Little Leagues to the Big Leagues. These are simple and proven techniques that have worked for the competitive youth league pitcher as well as the high-profile professional. This system shows you what goes through the mind of successful professional pitchers that make them exceptionally good. The inner secrets include their preparation, physical conditioning, and mental toughness. Pitchers who pay attention to every detail of the game, especially the small ones, will lead them to become winners.

In my long career at the professional level, I have noticed that the great pitchers have traits in common. What are those traits? It's their internal grit, drive, desire, work ethic, enthusiasm, and being a perfectionist that leads them to reach for higher sights. No matter how successful they've been, they still want to learn and apply something new, which in turn will make them better. When they get through their days, they are physically and more importantly mentally drained. They work so hard on the craft that when they are in the middle of the competition, their minds are so engaged that at games end, they are mentally spent.

CHAPTER 1

History of Pitching and Mechanics

Throughout the history of baseball, we have seen many changes from the early stages until the present when it comes to pitching and mechanics. Historically, we can compare the initial way pitchers threw the baseball to how players in other sports throw different objects. Take javelin throwers, for example, they run at a decent speed to get momentum, but as they prepare to make the javelin throw, they have a controlled movement to their backside to gather energy to produce an explosive launch on a flat ground surface. By having a controlled backside gathering, they have a linear direction and finish through the release of that javelin. Shot putters are the same. They gain momentum on their first drive, and as they get to their second power position, they are entirely leveraged over their back foot, and all the energy derives from that which is sustaining all his weight, and then explodes into release and full extension.

I like to use another comparison: Picture someone knocking down a coconut off a tree with a rock. Would you run towards the tree and have forward momentum without getting any leverage off our backside? Or, as you are ready to throw the rock, would you gather yourself to your backside for power and leverage to throw the rock, to knock that coconut off the tree? The answer: get on your backside for maximum force to throw the rock and have a linear direction and momentum through the release of the rock to the coconut. The shoulder and belt angles created to throw the rock should be the same angles used to throw as the pitcher is going down the slope. When most pitchers from the early days pitched, they had big hand movements, hands down by their thighs continuing behind towards 2nd base. Then those hands were lifted over their heads as they stepped behind the rubber. They transitioned their weight to step forward with the power foot, followed by the leg lifted diagonally to the opposite pectoral muscle, and hips led their direction as they went into high leg kicks to the plate, causing their head to stay over the back foot and rubber creating great momentum and leverage from their lower half. When pitchers like Lefty Grove, Lefty Gomez, Red Ruffing, Bob Feller, Satchel Paige, Sandy Koufax, Warren Spann, and Juan Marichal stepped behind the rubber, all their weight was on that back foot. They would then pivot with the power foot feeling for the rubber, then high leg kicks, and as their hips and lower half led, the head would be completely over the back foot, allowing the arm the necessary time to get into position to throw and make a pitch. These mechanics were the customary way most pitchers pitched in that day and age. * **See figures 1-1 to 1-15**

In those early years, MLB teams had a four-man starting rotation with only three days' rest throughout the season. Some pitchers logged 300 plus innings a year with no known pitch counts. They also didn't have the luxury of a closer, a set-up man, and situational pitchers. The famous modern day saying of five and dive did not exist. They were the best pitchers on the staff, and they pitched until their arms were tired, or they were no longer effective. Juan Marichal once hooked up with Warren Spann at Candlestick Park and went 16 innings against each other, with Marichal getting the win 1-0. Marichal threw 227 pitches an average of 14.18 pitches per inning in beating the Braves 1-0 on July 2, 1963. Spahn threw 201 in that game averaging 12.56 pitches per inning. Marichal once threw 30 complete games in a season. Warren Spahn was an iron man by the time he carried his shutout into the 16th inning at Candlestick Park. The left-hander led the National League in complete games nine times over his career, including three straight times after his 40th birthday.

Every pitcher that throws a baseball has his quirks on how he does it. In that era, most pitchers seemed to mirror each other. They had the same movements. Many pitchers had long careers and stayed healthy for as long as they pitched. So, what did they do differently than the modern-day pitchers to last throwing that many innings, and so many pitches?

The modern-day pitcher has so much more information on biomechanics, science, technology, video analysis, and coaching knowledge. The million-dollar question is why do we have so many injuries? Shouldn't it be the other way around? Injuries should be minimized, not breaking historical record numbers. If the modern-day pitcher has limited innings and pitch counts, why so many injuries? It just doesn't make any sense.

Below is a study on injured pitchers from the 1950s through the year 2004.

Year	No. Of Pitchers	Pitchers on DL	% Of Pitchers on DL
1953	154	5	3
1959	195	14	7
1964	221	38	17
1972	263	62	24
1981	330	165	50
1992	462	313	68
2004	342	248	73

Carl Reid, Library of Congress Consultation. [1]

The pitching coaches became part of Major League Baseball in the 1920s. However, in the early 1950s and prior, the pitching coaches were former catchers. In the mid to late 1950s, they made the transition to former pitchers to lead the staff as pitching coaches.[2]

In the 1970s the pitching coaches started to get more involved with the mechanics of the pitchers. Pitching coaches began to try and simplify the delivery. Many ideas began to evolve from using towel drills, shortening stride length, getting the hand out of the glove earlier, pitching from the opposite side of the mound if they threw across their body, and the rocker step in front of the rubber. The terms like flying open, rushing, speeding up, and stay back, came to life. We also heard the term cloning, and because there were so many different interpretations of how the delivery was supposed to be, a lot of contradictory views started to take place. By adding the term "cloning," coaches and organizations at the professional level let pitchers throw a certain way, and then tried to correct the issue by using Band-Aids--a quick fix to a long-term mechanical deficiency. Today, there are different methods on how a long-toss program or weighted balls will enhance arm strength. If the pitcher stops doing the long toss or weighted ball program, would the pitcher maintain his velocity? In the past, one Major League organization had their pitchers throughout their system throw footballs as part of the throwing program. Another organization had their pitchers throw long toss as far as they could go and having their throwing partner stay in one spot to receive the ball before their bullpens and games. If his throwing partner moves from throw to throw, the pitcher was farther out than his maximum comfortable distance, or out of his range. Pitchers made many unnecessary or non-competitive throws, which did not enhance their ability to get hitters out. After making these long-distance throws, the pitcher is then asked to make pitches at the bottom of the strike zone in the game 20 minutes later.

These programs have produced an alarmingly high rate of elbow and shoulder injuries. So, what are the issues that are facing us? How do we cut down on the injuries? Many of these young pitchers' first coaches are parents. How many of these first teams they joined were coached by a parent of one of the players, or a former pitcher that might have played at a higher level, such as college or professional, and decided they wanted to coach. They primarily use our kids as guinea pigs to develop their apprenticeship learning curve.

In professional baseball, each team has their way of teaching the delivery. Every organization has its unique way of showing their pitchers their system from all doing it the same method called cloning, or each pitcher has his way of doing his delivery without coaches tinkering much with it. They all have a throwing program they want each pitcher to replicate, and long toss throwing programs vary from organization to organization.

There are great pitchers with great deliveries today who simulate the early day pitchers. They do not step behind the rubber or go over their heads with their hands. They do not have high leg kicks etc., but they have the same basic principles. Felix Hernandez, John Lester, Nolan Ryan, Ron Guidry, Clayton Kershaw, Pedro Martinez, and Mariano Rivera to name a few of the pitchers that have similarities when we compare them to the greats of the past. These pitchers look like they are moving in slow motion, but the release of the baseball is fast, and it's very deceptive to hitters. They stay back in their deliveries so well, and with linear movement, they get closer to hitters at the release point, making it harder for them to pick up pitches which translates into 2 to 3 mph illusionary velocity. It merely means that it looks faster to the naked eye than it is to the hitter as it registers on the radar gun. It's a perfect example as to why Mariano Rivera pitched with one pitch, the cutter. It's because he released the ball closer to the hitter causing them to pick the ball up late, and

20

therefore, the last bit of late movement caused havoc on Major League hitters during his illustrious career. Kenley Jansen is another pitcher in the Major Leagues who released the baseball closest to the hitter, and he has had Mariano Rivera type success during his brief time as a closer with the same pitch, the cutter. Late release point closer to the hitter is a byproduct of a pitcher doing all the little things early in his delivery to achieve the result of an excellent full extension, giving the best deception any pitcher can have.

Unleash the Pitcher in You will introduce the Levers Method in this system. The idea is to bring awareness globally to all inspiring young pitchers as well as to those who are competing at the professional levels, and to all coaches and parents. We want to address to pitchers that their objective should be how easy I can throw hard. Usually, you throw harder when you are not trying. Stabilization of your back foot on the rubber is the first vital part of your delivery. A wobbly foot is un-stabilized. Your upper body should never outrun your lower half. It should be the other way around -- your lower half out running your upper body. You should see the body coming precisely--the lower half (legs) first and then the arm. The lower half simulates the handle of a whip and then arm acts like the whip itself as it snaps out front. We will show you how pitchers accomplish linear direction to avoid falling to either side of the mound and explain how staying closed with the front side has everything to do with how you use the backside which will lead pitchers to understand that a leveraged delivery gets the most power out of your body to get the best arm speed, and in turn will give you, your best fastball. Unleash The Pitcher In You objective is not only to teach pitchers the correct way of delivering a baseball but also cover every aspect of the game. We will go over the hitter's game plans and approaches, controlling the running game at both 1st and 2nd base, fielding your position, your responsibilities as you prepare for games, and much more. A pitcher is a special bread of athlete who is willing to do everything to be the best he can be. In baseball, the pitcher always has the spotlight shining on him, and if he takes things for granted on the mound, it can be a very lonely place.

However, on the other hand, when we prepare to the best of our capabilities, a pitcher's mound is the best place to be on that baseball field. We are the general, the captain, and the leader on our team. Pitchers set the tone that will give their team the best chances to win the game, and we at HLB will show you how all the little things lead to the big things, and that's winning baseball games. If you are ready, then we are excited to take you on our pitching journey.

OUR PITCHING PIONEERS 1

THEY STARTED WITH HANDS TOGETHER WHILE GETTING THEIR SIGNS.

Figure 1-1

OUR PITCHING PIONEERS 2

AS THEY STEPPED BACK, THEY WOULD DROP AND SEPERATE THEIR HANDS AROUND THEIR LOWER THIGH.

Figure 1-2

OUR PITCHING PIONEERS 3

AS THEY CONTINUED TO STEP BEHIND WITH LIFT LEG THEIR ARMS WOULD START TO GAIN MOMENTUM WITH A PENDULUM TYPE OF UPWARD MOVEMENT

Figure 1-3

OUR PITCHING PIONEERS 4

THEY CREATED A FLUID UP & DOWN SWING OF THE ARMS BUILDING MOMENTUM TO COUNTER THE LEG LIFT

ALL THEIR WEIGHT TRANSFERRED ONTO THEIR LIFT LEG

Figure 1-4

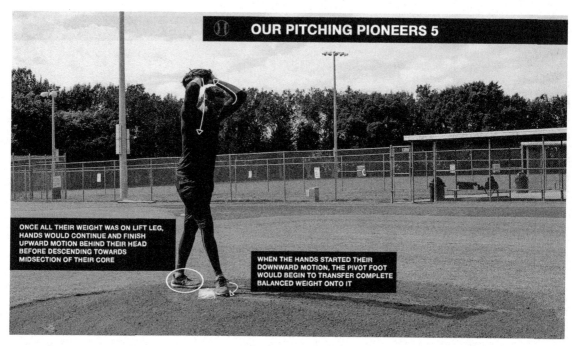

Figure 1-5

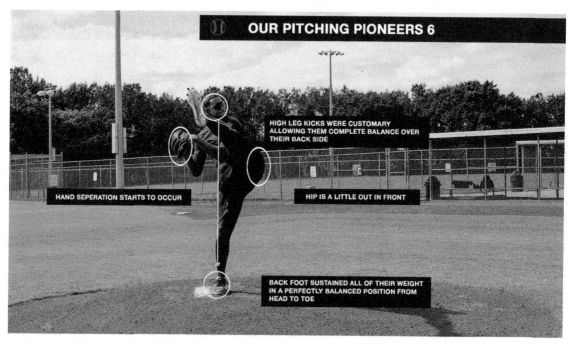

Figure 1-6

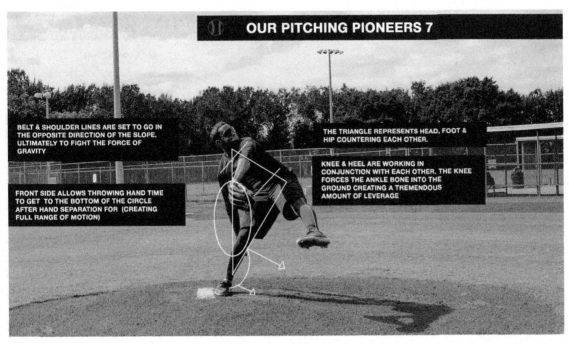

Figure 1-7

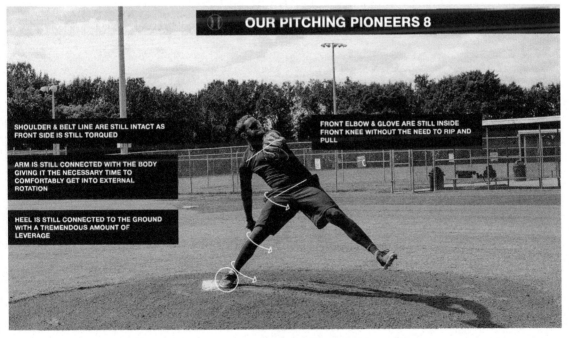

Figure 1-8

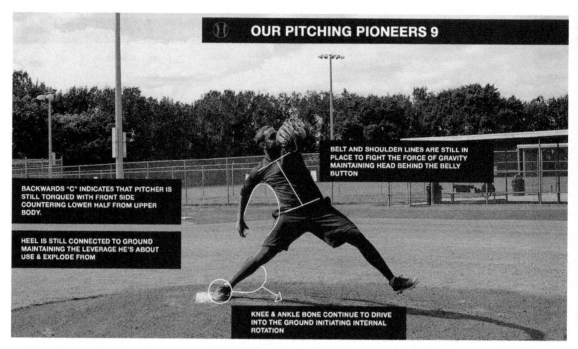

OUR PITCHING PIONEERS 9

BELT AND SHOULDER LINES ARE STILL IN PLACE TO FIGHT THE FORCE OF GRAVITY MAINTAINING HEAD BEHIND THE BELLY BUTTON

BACKWARDS "C" INDICATES THAT PITCHER IS STILL TORQUED WITH FRONT SIDE COUNTERING LOWER HALF FROM UPPER BODY.

HEEL IS STILL CONNECTED TO GROUND MAINTAINING THE LEVERAGE HE'S ABOUT USE & EXPLODE FROM

KNEE & ANKLE BONE CONTINUE TO DRIVE INTO THE GROUND INITIATING INTERNAL ROTATION

Figure 1-9

OUR PITCHING PIONEERS 10

ARM (THREE LEVERS) GET INTO EXTERNAL ROTATION WITH EASE

GLOVE HANDS STAYS COMFORTABLY INSIDE INSIDE OF FRONT KNEE STAYING ON LINE WITH TARGET

HEEL FINALLY DISENGAGES FROM THE GROUND AS THE BALL OF THE FOOT & TOES DRIVE CREATING LINEAR ROTATION OF LOWER HALF BRINGING HEEL TO THE OUTSIDE OF THE TOES

BACK HIP & KNEE INTERNALLY ROTATE TO START DELIVERING THE TRUNK

Figure 1-10

Figure 1-11

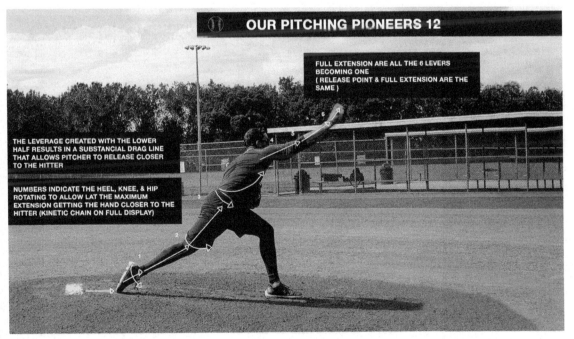

Figure 1-12

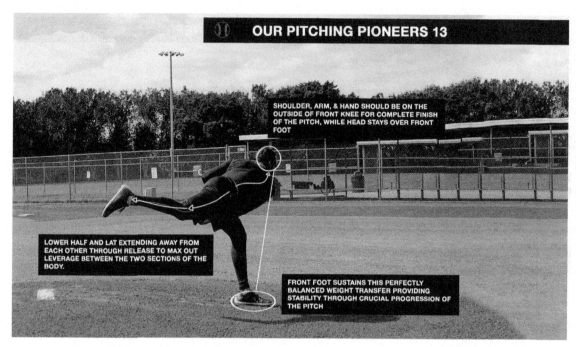

Figure 1-13

Figure 1-14

Figure 1-15

CHAPTER 2

Levers Method-Pitching Delivery Checkpoints

Pitchers Check Points

1. Rocker Step: To build momentum by stepping back behind the rubber on an angle.
    1. Stabilize foot on the rubber - (Hooking spikes on rubber is a recommended option)
    2. Balance – Knee lift and glove should raise diagonally to opposite chest
    3. Allows hip to be in front of the rest of the body
    4. Rolling of the hips mounts pitcher on backside down to the heel and sets belt and shoulder lines

Simultaneous Triangles
    a. 1st Triangle-Head, Back foot, and front hip.
    b. 2nd Triangle-Glove hand, ball hand, and lead leg are fully extended, after hand separation.
    c. Hand separation or dumping of hands over the rubber as hips lead forward. The pitcher maintains shoulder and belt lines diagonally.

2. Backward "C" is the position one sees after separation from the ball to the backfoot. (It allows the pitcher to use his legs better and longer down the slope)

Torque-Staying on backward C allows the front shoulder to stay back in the fascia-X while glove side firms up after inward shoulder roll towards the 3rd base side if you're right-handed, and the 1st base side if you're a left-handed pitcher.

3. Wall of Resistance - Front side comes to a complete stop as front foot strike so that the backside can explode, and shoulder can allow throwing arm to get through front knee and continue past it, finishing with shoulder and arm to be on the outside of the landing knee. All the weight wraps around the front heel and ankle on the complete finish.

4. We do not teach to lock from the knee at release as it prevents finishing fluidly and limits how much closer to the hitter the release gets and allows the pitcher to land in a good fielding position.[3]

Checkpoints are in place to simplify a pitcher's mind into seeing pictures that he can translate into positions of his delivery without becoming mechanical. Checkpoints should be fluid and in perfect sequence from start to finish during the throwing motion. When seeing a pitcher that has an awkward delivery, it merely means that from a Kinesiology point of view something in his timing is off, just like watching a person dance off rhythm or offbeat. The body has a way of adjusting to anything, so we see short cuts to release point with shorter arm action, or levers to get to the same point as pitchers with smooth deliveries. * **See figure 2-1**

Starting from the wind up we recommend having a pitcher step back on an angle behind the rubber to keep his head over the backside easier. All the weight should be over the hip and foot as he steps back with basically having very little to no pressure on the power foot. We see many pitchers look like they are tippy-toeing or tapping with the ball of the foot at this point of delivery which is done to keep the head back slightly behind the pitcher's power foot before pivoting to get alongside the rubber or to hook the rubber with spikes with ease. Today's pitchers are taught to step to the side of the rubber not realizing that their head is slightly in front of their power foot, and gravity can affect the pitcher by initiating the upper half prematurely, causing the kinetic chain to get out of whack immediately, and gravity controlling the delivery instead of the pitcher controlling the gravity. We encourage pitchers to hook the rubber with outside cleats off spikes to create stronger foot position, and initiate leverage with the inner part of the leg, and direction towards the plate will be much easier. It is not mandatory, but we recommend it to have good direction towards the plate. Foot stabilization and use of the whole foot to have a good direction towards the plate including the heel is vital for the use of lower half. * **See figure 2-2**

In some cases, we recommend a pitcher lock his knee on leg lift to feel his heel and the rest of the foot, which is the only body part connected to the ground. He will feel connected from the back hip down through the knee to the heel, which for the pitcher will translate into initiating the hips and lower half power easier and better. It is essential for a pitcher to think of having a flexible back hip not to be inclined to collapse the back knee which is the point where a pitcher will automatically set shoulder and belt lines in a diagonal angle. Pitching coaches need to be aware of the pitcher not dropping his back shoulder behind the back hip because their hips set the shoulder and belt lines. If a pitcher drops back the shoulder or leans too far back, he will be in a weak or unleveraged position. * **See figure 2-3**

As pitchers' hips start to go forward, hand separation naturally happens slightly behind the back hip. We call this dumping the hands. It is the point in which the hand comes out of the glove and having time to get to the bottom of what we call the circle. It is a crucial stage because the arm is made up of three levers. Shoulder to elbow is one, elbow to wrist is two, and wrist to fingertips is the third. Many injuries occur due to not giving these levers time to get into the throwing position and compromises the ligaments and tendons by stretching which starts with the pectoral muscles pulling away from the shoulder, and the elbow follows suit. This stretching of the shoulder and elbow happens when the power leg does not have time to start the rotation. As the belt and shoulder lines set, the pitcher will transition into his backward "C." * **See figure 2-4**

Good power pitchers stay in this backward-C position longer down the slope than most other pitchers who don't throw as hard. This position creates a tremendous amount of torque between the upper and lower half. The backward-C is the position that leverages or doesn't leverage a pitcher. At this point of the delivery, the head is directly above the belly button or slightly behind causing the back leg to have all the leverage to begin the rotation from the ground up. It is a two-piece throw between the lower body followed by the upper body. * **See figure 2-5**

The kinetic chain is in perfect sequence to begin the rotation that is perfectly synchronized to initiate a powerful throw or pitch. It also allows him to work against the slope and gravity because the belt and shoulder lines are still diagonal, and not parallel to the ground, creating an enormous amount of energy at foot strike initiating the linear rotation that is spoken about so often but rarely understood on how this action is created and done.

There are two types of rotations: one is stationary, and the other is linear. The one all pitchers should strive for is the linear rotation because that means the pitcher has done all the kinetic movements we have broken down and can stay through the pitch and allow him to finish in a solid fielding position. To get the maximum use of your legs, we need to stay in our backward C down the slope if possible. By doing so, it will keep a pitcher's front foot and hip from trying to prematurely open and again cause the kinetic chain to start with the front lower half side. As a pitcher, it will allow you to store the most energy by working against the slope fighting against the gravity that is pulling you down. A pitcher will have created more power, which leads to more explosiveness at the release point or full extension. * **See figure 2-6**

Remember we are working against the gravity as it is pulling us down. We fight against the slope to give your arm more time to comfortably and consistently get the ball out of glove down and up, and then to your release point, consequently, commanding the baseball. We have been able to have pitchers take classroom sessions to bring awareness so they can maximize their leverage. * **See figure 2-7**

Pitchers who have had long careers and have sustained great success did similar things. Covering the checkpoints is the start of having them understand what they need to adjust in their delivery so they can repeat their release point consistently, especially in games.

The next step is taking them on the practice mounds to work on their mechanical checkpoints. Each pitcher has his idiosyncrasies. Putting pitchers through drills is the most effective way to get pitchers to adjust and change whatever deficiency they have in their mechanics. Drills are the new construction pitchers need to go through. Imagine driving on a highway to get to your destination, mind and body are used to navigate that route. We must construct a new road for the brain and muscles to adjust and create new brain and muscle cohesiveness as the term used loosely is muscle memory. That new construction are drills. The drills consist of going through their delivery with a towel for resistance at release point. Doing the mechanics in front of a mirror is a powerful tool. Doing the delivery from behind the mound on an upward slope promotes shoulder and belt lines. The behind the mound drill will also reinforce the backward "C" controlling and keeping the head over your backside or torqued longer, to give you an explosive finish and follow through.

Doing the mechanics with eyes closed is a powerful tool as well. Eyes closed drills will enhance visualization and imagery. There are two types of visualization-- external and internal. Internal is going through the delivery and feeling it. External is watching you do it. The more powerful of the two is internal.

Figure 2-1

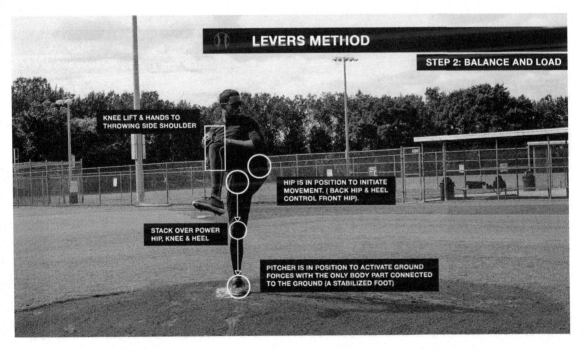

Figure 2-2

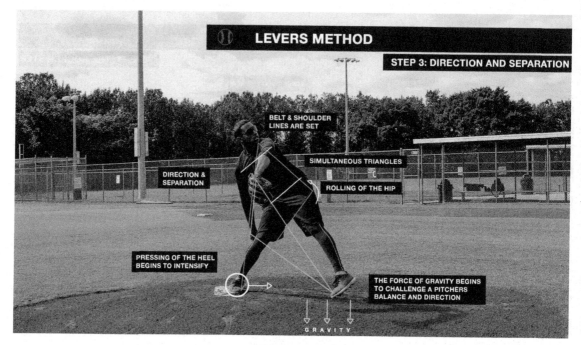

Figure 2-3

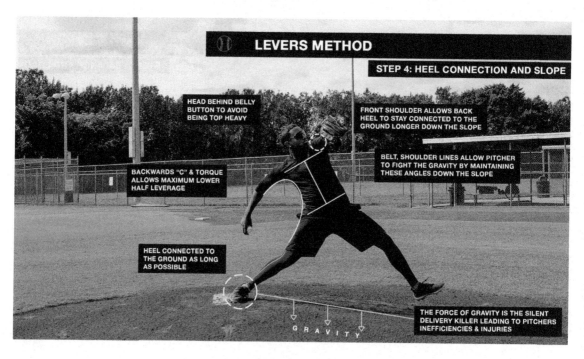

Figure 2-4

Figure 2-5

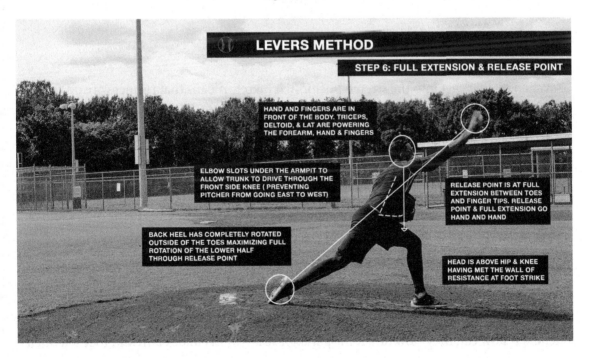

Figure 2-6

Figure 2-7

Pitching from the Stretch

When pitchers get into the stretch position, it merely means that runners are on the base unless the pitcher pitches from the stretch all the time. In this case, we'll assimilate runners on base. The stretch position is the part of the game in which a pitcher gets tested in all facets of his abilities. The game of baseball is a game of advancement from an offensive standpoint where runners are always trying to get to that extra base. The pitchers must be efficient at preventing runners from stealing a base while keeping his focus on the hitter.

He must be able to deliver the ball in 1.3 seconds or less to give his catcher a chance to throw potential base stealers out at 2nd and 3rd base. He must vary his hold times to the plate or attempt a pickoff to 1st base. He must develop the patience to hold the ball without pitching, or attempt pickoff throws to 1st base in 4 seconds or longer. A key question for pitchers is how can they slow down the game? The answer is to be calm and focused during the pressure situations the game presents to us.

The pitcher must always have his mechanical checkpoints in place, which apply from the stretch as well as from the wind-up. * **See figure 2-8**

When a pitcher gets his sign from the catcher, he should immediately turn from the waist towards 1st base and pick up the base runner and see where his lead is. * **See figure 2-9**

After gathering that information, he comes to his set position without taking his eyes off the runner, checking to see if the runner takes another half to full step to counter it with a quick pickoff attempt. Some base runners get late leads by standing on the bag until the pitcher has received his sign and is about to come set. When the pitcher comes set, his feet should be a little closer than shoulder-width. * **See figure 2-10**

The reason is we try to start the lower half first, and if the feet are far apart, he must get back to a balanced position and can cause the pitcher valuable time and start down the slope with front side prematurely. The objective is to get the front hip started immediately and be on the backside creating the pitcher's best leverage. When the feet are too far apart, it causes the head to be in front of the rubber, and that causes a pitcher to rush right from the knee lift. We always should keep in mind that the force of the gravity plays a big role in a pitcher's delivery. Once the front knee lift occurs, it should be passing the back knee as the pitcher is rolling the front hip. The weight will cause the pitcher to go directly on the power side to start direction towards the plate. We are driving with the back hip to prevent chasing the front hip down the slope. * **See figure 2-11**

The idea is to drive off the stabilized foot on the rubber causing that front hip to lead the way. If we use the ground, then it stands to reason that the power foot controls the movement, which in sequential order is foot, knee, hips, torso, shoulder, elbow, wrist and fingertips. We dump the hands behind our back hip, allowing the front side automatically to stay back, allowing hand separation to happen and give time for the throwing hand to get to the bottom of the circle with ease. At this point of the delivery, the throwing hand will get fully extended down to the mid to lower thigh area of your power leg which is the part of the delivery where the simultaneous triangles happen. * **See figure 2-12**

At this point, the shoulder and belt lines are set. A way for a pitcher to feel the ground and drive off the back foot is to lock his power knee or back knee to feel his drive off the back heel immediately. The pitcher will feel completely connected from the hip down to the heel for a power drive to the plate. When the pitcher leads with the hips, and the head stays back, he will be in the backward "C" down the slope. The knee of the power leg will begin to flex forward in a downward angle to get leverage from the ground after it was locked.

When a pitcher stays in his backward "C" long enough, his head will stay behind his belly button as his hips are working down the slope. If he can do this, he will be in a very leveraged position because his back leg will be the body part loading all the force and power. We call this being in his best torque position. The torque position is when just before the front foot strikes, the lower half is still closed, but ready to explode and the upper body from the waist up is still somewhat gathered and twisted or torqued inside of the front knee. * **See figure 2-13**

When a pitcher does this, he will allow his levers to get in position to throw the baseball, basically the slingshot position, which is when the hand and elbow are parallel to the ground (external rotation or layback position) and get a tremendous amount of leverage and power with complete circular arm action taking place. At this point, a pitcher's arm will look like it's moving in slow motion, with the only thing looking fast is the release point and the baseball coming at the hitter. We, as pitching coaches, believe in a linear rotation. What and how do you create linear rotation? The answer lies in the ability for the pitcher to start his delivery with his hips acting like the handle of a whip, which starts the action, and then the whip follows. The lower half is the handle of the whip, and the arm is the whip itself. Lower half first then the trunk and the arm second. When this linear movement happens, the pitchers have ample time to have hand, fingers, behind and on top of the baseball on release creating a natural downhill plane when pitches cross the strike zone. Full extension and release point are the same things.

A pitcher feels like he releases the ball out in front, but the reality is that the baseball comes out with the hand slightly behind the elbow to full extension. The last piece comes on follow-through where the pitcher finishes with his shoulder, arm, and hand on the outside of the landing knee. This position creates an X between the throwing arm and landing leg. The power leg finish should be on the side or slightly in front of the pitcher to transition to a solid fielding position. * **See figure 2-14**

As the pitcher finishes his follow through the front of his stride foot lifts a bit like all the weight kind of corkscrews onto the front heel. That is when a pitcher knows he has finished and maximized his delivery from beginning to end.

Figure 2-8

Figure 2-9

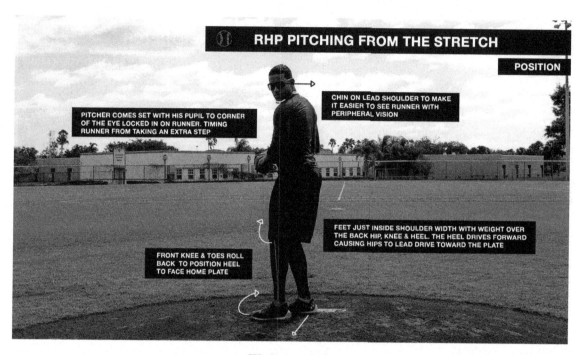

RHP PITCHING FROM THE STRETCH

POSITION

CHIN ON LEAD SHOULDER TO MAKE IT EASIER TO SEE RUNNER WITH PERIPHERAL VISION

PITCHER COMES SET WITH HIS PUPIL TO CORNER OF THE EYE LOCKED IN ON RUNNER. TIMING RUNNER FROM TAKING AN EXTRA STEP

FEET JUST INSIDE SHOULDER WIDTH WITH WEIGHT OVER THE BACK HIP, KNEE & HEEL. THE HEEL DRIVES FORWARD CAUSING HIPS TO LEAD DRIVE TOWARD THE PLATE

FRONT KNEE & TOES ROLL BACK TO POSITION HEEL TO FACE HOME PLATE

Figure 2-10

RHP PITCHING FROM THE STRETCH

STRETCH/ KNEE LIFT

THE KNEE LIFT SHOULD BE FRONT KNEE TO BACK KNEE. IN OTHER WORDS KNEE TO KNEE. SHORTER MOVEMENTS RATHER THAN BIGGER MOVEMENTS FROM THE WINDUP, BEING QUICKER TO THE PLATE

THE KINETIC CHAIN PROPERLY WORKING FROM GROUND UP, BACK HEEL, KNEE, HIP

BACK HEEL DRIVES FORWARD AND STARTS THE KINETIC CHAIN FROM THE GROUND UP TO BACK KNEE & HIP

Figure 2-11

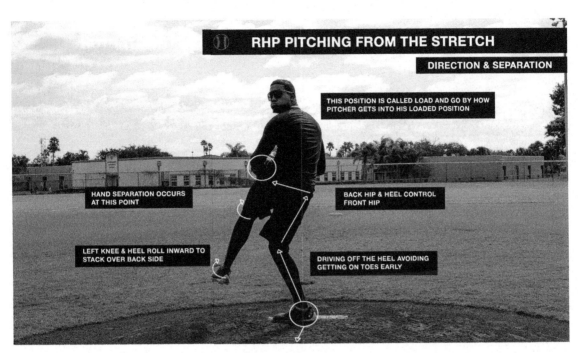

Figure 2-12

Figure 2-13

Figure 2-14

CHAPTER 3

Drills to Overcome Mechanical Flaws

Pitchers all have their idiosyncrasies about their mechanics. We can teach two pitchers to do the very same movements, but they will not look the same when they do them. Just like hitters have different ways of hitting, they still have the same principles in place. But hitters will not look the same when they are hitting except when we see still shot photos. Pitchers are the same regarding the principles. The pitcher's principles are Balance-Load/ Direction/Separation/Release point/Finish. These principles are covered in our formula of Rocker step/Stabilize foot on rubber/Balance/Simultaneous Triangles/Backward C/ Torque/Wall of Resistance etcetera.

We should picture ourselves driving down a highway on our way to work each day -- the route that gets us to our destination. The way a pitcher does his delivery is his route, and we ought to picture us constructing a new highway for his muscle memory or brain memory to get used to the new route, which will be his new delivery. Doing drills is the way to construct the new highway, and with the right ones, a pitcher can rectify any mechanical flaw.

One of the most critical parts of the delivery is where the pitcher's head is at leg lift or when he is set in the stretch position. Most pitchers have their head in front of the back foot, and that initiates him down the slope prematurely creating the universal term (rushing).

When in the stretch and hands come together, we need to look for, and see, the position of the pitcher's head. Many pitchers have their head in front of the back foot causing the same rushing effect. I use an indicator to show the pitcher where his head is in relation to his back leg on the rubber. I have pitcher come to his set position, then take my finger and draw a straight line starting at the middle of his head, which is the nose and proceed down the spinal cord, and continue down to the ground marking a line in the dirt which will show the pitcher how much in front of his back foot he actually is. I then have the pitcher inch by inch bring the front foot closer to the back foot until the pitcher feels he's completely standing over the back hip, knee, and foot without leaning. Now he's in a great position to start the hips correctly with his best leverage from the ground on up.

One of the pieces we work on is when lifting the knee, do it towards your back shoulder, pectoral muscle or hip. We should coordinate and match our hands with the knee at this point. The pitcher should feel a slight torque between the lower half and upper body. The front hip is also in front of the rest of the body when in this position. The beautiful thing is that the pitcher will feel all his weight solely on the back leg, which is what we need from him for power purposes. We must get him used to this position until it becomes second nature. Coaches from the stretch, when a pitcher comes to his set position make sure his feet are not too far apart (a little less than shoulder-width is ideal) which will give you an indication of where his head is at this point. We are trying to get the hips started early down the slope, and it's vital that his head is over his back foot for belt and shoulder lines to be set. By being in this position and working against the slope from the first movement, it will prevent the pitcher from being pulled down by the gravity. Working against gravity will create more energy and more energy translates into more power. The hips will get started late if the head is out front of the back foot causing the pitcher to take a short cut with the arm, or simply be late to release point. Back foot stabilization and feel, is another vital point. Have the pitcher lock out his back knee at full leg lift and ask him to have a flexible back hip. As he gets that back hip started because his back knee is locked, the pitcher will feel his heel from the back hip down to the ground feeling backside complete power and drive. The only body part connected to the ground is the back foot and it will have the most leverage because of this simple technique. The flexing of the back knee happens once he begins to move forward getting in front of the back foot which causes the ankle bone to tilt towards the dirt initiating the explosive rotation of knee to hip.

1. Stride out drill. The stride out drill is a way to have a pitcher emphasize the use of his back leg. He will focus on throwing the ball by initiating backside rotation. Make sure his stride is not too far apart. If he does, he will be off-balance and will lack power. His feet should be at a closer stride length than the one he has in games. The idea here is for him to maximize the use of his back leg and get over the front side. The chest should finish over the front knee with the shoulder and arm on the outside of that same knee. His back foot will sustain all his body weight when he loads and should have his heel on the outside of the toe with the laces of the shoe facing the ground when he finishes his throw. Make sure he doesn't lift that back foot off the ground after the throw. He will start with his feet spread and hands at set position ball in the glove. * **See figures 3-1, 3-2, 3-3**

Load back making sure lead shoulder gets behind the front hip and use the back leg to do the work until he gets to full extension, which is the distance between back foot and fingertips at release point. * **See figures 3-4 to 3-6**

Release point and full extension mean the same thing. What is the full extension? It is his release point. And what is his release point? It is the full extension. If done correctly, you should feel the ball come out of your hand with life, showing you how strong and vital the use of your lower half is. A pitcher can do this drill as part of his initial throwing program daily. The stride out drill can also be done off the mound for both touch and feel and regular 60' 6" throws with catcher down in catching position. The turn and dump hands drill will teach you how to use the upper body when throwing a baseball. To start the drill, each pitcher will be facing each other, and feet spread side to side but making sure that his lead foot is slightly in front of the power foot. With the ball in glove, the pitcher takes his glove side shoulder and turns it towards throwing side chest. As he turns that shoulder, the glove hand will be facing up and then he dumps the ball out of glove with the thumb facing down breaking at the wrist. That is called dumping the hands. Most of your body weight is loaded on the power side. Allow full range of motion of throwing the hand to do its full circle and make the throw using and staying on your power side through release. The turn and dump drill can be incorporated at the beginning of your daily throwing program.

2. Behind the mound uphill throwing. This drill is perfect to work on your belt and shoulder lines. When in your regular pitching delivery, we initiate the lower half, and this drill will re-enforce this to happen. By going uphill behind the mound, you will re-enforce the direction you will be going when you are making pitches to the plate, and that is as you're fighting against the gravity which will buy you time for your arm to get into throwing position. You can start from the wind-up or stretch position and the catcher will be in front of the plate and down. * **See figure 3-7**

This drill also re-enforces the use of your backside and linear rotation through the front side. Keep in mind your focus and concentration should be getting each pitch to the bottom of the zone. * **See figures 3-8 to 3-12**

3. **Towel Drills**. This drill helps pitchers feel resistance at release point. We can only throw a baseball but so many times and this drill will help you work on your delivery without the intensity that throwing a baseball has. We recommend the pitcher puts his middle and index fingers at the middle of the towel and drapes both sides evenly which will emulate the fingers on a baseball. If he pitches from both the wind-up and stretch, he can work on each delivery--20 to 25 repetitions are enough for a daily routine. Watch not to go 100% as 60% to 70% effort is ideal. The idea is to feel the delivery with a nice fluid motion. A coach or a partner can be in front of the slope and see where it is that his extension point is and have his glove out in that spot for him to hit it and repeat. It has been said that towel drills are not the same as throwing a baseball and we agree. The intensity pitchers use to throw a baseball is far greater than a fluid motion with a towel in which the arm will not reach the measurements or go as far back to external rotation or finish on follow through to the internal rotation the same. While this is true, the benefits of this drill are valuable. The pitcher is just basically feeling extension. He can close the gap between the knee and the opposite chest, resulting in the best follow through the pitcher can achieve. And lastly, many young pitchers try and throw hard as soon as they begin to separate ball out of the glove instead of at release point, which is where they feel the towel snap out front.

4. **Mirror Drills**. Working in front of a mirror is where a pitcher can internalize his delivery. A coach can point out what to work on, or he can simply watch himself repeat his delivery after working on the other drills. He can work from the wind-up or the stretch based on his positioning. He can use the towel as well to feel the resistance at release point.

Note: A pitcher needs to continually work on his delivery in order not to have to think about it in games. All this work is done so when you are competing you rely on hand-eye coordination and execute your game plan. Mechanical work is merely to be done in the body shop when you can segment your delivery and emphasize what part you need to improve to make you a better pitcher. Every part you master is like going after your black belt in Karate in martial arts. Be a master of your delivery.

STRIDE OUT DRILL W/ COACH 1

PITCHER STARTS WITH HANDS EVENLY POSITIONED ON THE MIDDLE OF HIS BODY

FEET SHOULD NOT BE TOO FAR APART TO MAXIMIZE LEVERAGE OF BACKSIDE. WE'RE TRYING TO DEVELOP AS MUCH POWER WITH OUR LOWER HALF AS WE POSSIBLY CAN

Figure 3-1

STRIDE OUT DRILL W/ COACH 2

HEAD IS BEHIND THE BELLY BUTTON ON THE LOAD SETTING SHOULDER AND BELT LINES, REINFORCING THE FIGHTING OF GRAVITY WHEN MAKING A PITCH

ARM GETS TO THE BOTTOM OF THE CIRCLE TO INITIATE FULL RANGE OF MOTION

TRANSITION WEIGHT BACK KEEPING KNEE INSIDE OF BACK FOOT. LEAD SHOULDER GETS BACK ENOUGH TO PUT ADDED WEIGHT ON BACK WHEEL

Figure 3-2

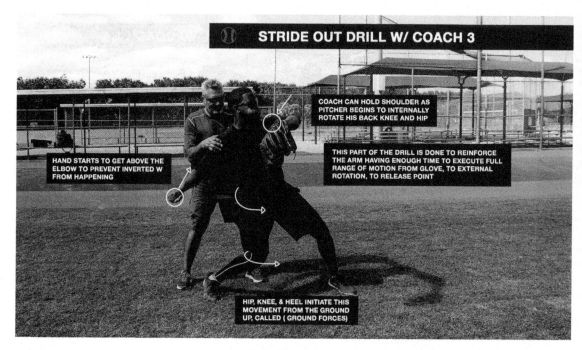

Figure 3-3

Figure 3-4

Figure 3-5

Figure 3-6

Figure 3-7

Figure 3-8

Figure 3-9

Figure 3-10

Figure 3-11

Figure 3-12

Eyes Closed Drills

Having a pitcher do drills with his eyes closed is a potent tool. As in the Drills to Correct Mechanical Flaws and segmenting, these drills can be used to construct the new highway we mentioned earlier, meaning, new muscle or brain memory. Having a pitcher do drills with his eyes closed will enhance his other senses and he'll be more in tune with the feel of his body. Remember when one of the senses is taken away from a human being, the other senses are enhanced. The pitcher's body parts must be in the right places for him to accomplish this. His learning curve will be much quicker to achieve a new way of muscle or brain memory with the new delivery.

When doing all the drills: stride out drill, turn and dump hands drill, behind the mound uphill throwing, towel drills, doing delivery without anything in hand on the mound. They can even throw a bullpen to a catcher making some pitches in the beginning with eyes closed and increasing the amount of pitches as they become more comfortable when the pitcher does their next bullpens. When doing bullpens, they will concentrate on the release point or full extension. They can throw a pitch with eyes open and then repeat it with eyes closed. These drills can be done keeping in mind that we must explain to the pitchers that for them to be completely balanced with eyes closed, they can concentrate on having the head, spinal cord, and belly button aligned in a straight line. If the head, spinal cord, and belly button are aligned, they will be able to run through these drills with ease. Their center of gravity starts at the belly button connecting lower half with the upper half. Their equilibrium will be intact allowing them to do the movements correctly and get the most out of every drill. To enhance a pitcher's mechanical flaw, he must stay in that backward C for as long as he can down the slope, and that is when the head, spine, and belly button are in a straight line for balance from beginning to end of delivery.

Eyes closed drills will enhance visualization and imagery. There are two types of visualization, external and internal. Internal is going through the delivery and feeling it. External is watching yourself doing your mechanics. The more powerful of the two is internal.

A pitcher can use visualization and mental imagery as a form of experience. The pitcher can start by visualizing the mound, the grass, home plate, the catcher's shoes, shin guards, the laces inside the catcher's glove, the light coming through his web. He can also envision the baseball, the seams, the Rawlings logo, making a well-located pitch, throwing your curveball or slider for strikes, expanding the zone in the dirt, and throwing your fastball on the black with two strikes. Visualize the batters you will be facing and pitch by pitch how you will get them out. Visualize yourself releasing the ball where you want to throw a quality strike. Picture being in a double play situation and making the pitch to get you out of the inning with a ball on the ground. Visualize having two strikes on the hitter and making that perfectly located pitch to strike the batter out. These are a few examples of how powerful visualization and mental imagery can be to take your focus and concentration to a whole new level if one applies it as part of your preparation.* **See figures 3-13 to 3-19**

EYES CLOSED DRILL

PITCHER STARTS WITH HIS EYES OPEN GETTING A VISUAL OF WHERE HE'S GOING TO THROW THE BALL

Figure 3-13

Figure 3-14

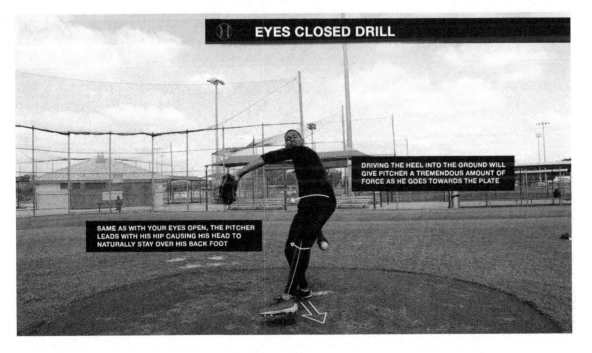

Figure 3-15

Figure 3-16

Figure 3-17

Figure 3-18

Figure 3-19

CHAPTER 4

LONG TOSS PROGRAM WITH COACH

When starting a long toss program, a pitcher should ask:

1. What is the benefit of this program?
2. Why and how far is an adequate distance?
3. Is this program going to give me more power or arm speed on pitches?
4. Will this program get me to throw more quality strikes?

In my journey instructing pitchers at the professional level, a long-toss program is a sensitive aspect of pitching. I'm committed to showing you the one I feel is the best to get the most out of your development as a pitcher. One of the priorities is to mechanically emulate the closest throw that matches your pitch off the mound. As with any pitch off the mound, we must start our lower half first in your long toss program, the hips will also initiate your throw.

1. Before making the throw, the pitcher should have his front shoulder facing his intended target. He should be in a set position just as he came set before making a pitch.
2. He will then take a step with the front foot driving off his back leg and crow hop behind front foot with his power foot.
3. As a pitcher is crossing behind the front foot with the power foot, his hands will separate out of the glove. It is crucial that he stays in his backward "C" as long as he can to get the most out of his back-power leg. The backward C is what creates the most leverage and allows the backside to initiate the throw from the ground up which will also give you the ability to have linear rotation staying through your throw at and after the release point.

4. When we see a pitcher pulling off, or flying open, or off-balance and falling off at the release point, it is because he wasn't in his backward "C" long enough to maximize the use of his power leg which throws off his balance and zaps him of his power.

5. An example is if you were going to throw your farthest throw, one would take an aggressive step towards where you are throwing, and the upper body would naturally get behind the lower half to get leverage and power. For some reason, a pitcher wants to go forward once on the mound and gravity starts to affect his natural way of making a strong solid throw. You are also going down a slope. We need to be working on going against the gravity in all our drills and throwing program.

6. Finally, we come to release and follow through. When everything is done correctly at the start, then it should fall like dominos in perfect sequence to get to this part of the throw. Full extension is the distance between the power foot and fingertips when releasing the baseball. The connection of the foot to the ground is vital as it promotes leverage and explosiveness on follow through. The chest should be very close to the front knee on your finish. Your throwing arm and shoulder should finish on the outside of the landing knee.

Figure 4-1

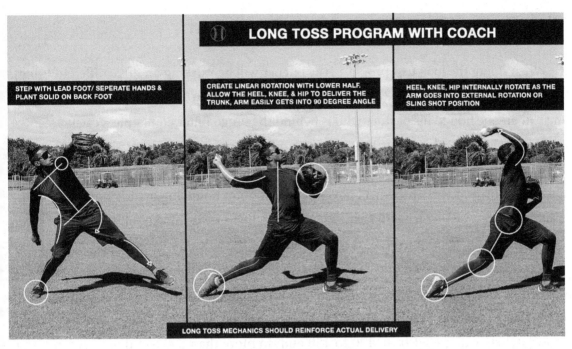

Figure 4-2

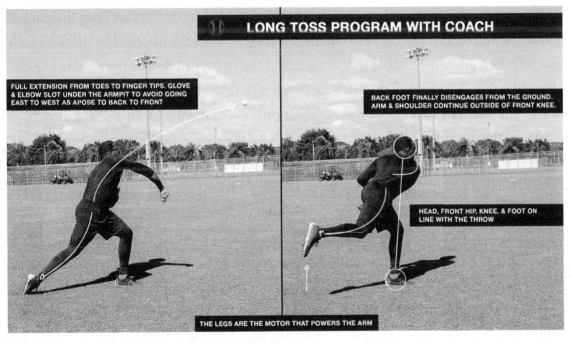

Figure 4-3

The Fungo Drill Throwing Program

When doing the long toss program, the pitcher will be working on three different things. First, he fields the ground ball then athletically does a crow hop (discussed earlier) and throws the ball on one hop to his partner who is behind the fungo hitter emulating a catcher.

The pitching coach will hit fungos to the pitcher in the outfield grass from either foul line starting at 60 feet. Pitcher gets loose slowly, but gradually moves back about three steps after each throw. Every throw will have the intention of bouncing it and coming up to the waist of the receiver which will keep re-enforcing the throw he makes off the mound when he pitches. It also helps the pitchers command by trying to hit the spot every time to get the perfect hop to the receiver. The coach can also put a towel, a rubber home plate, or a hat to give him a constant target and receiver should be positioned about 10 to 12 feet from that target that has been set up. The pitcher goes as far as he feels, but you will soon find out that most pitchers will go out from 120 to 150 and no more than 200 feet due to getting what they need out of these throws because of the pitcher one hopping their receiver. The idea is for them to use their legs and torso without putting any stress on the arm once the pitcher gets out to his comfortable distance and then works his way back to where he started which was at 60 feet. Once the pitcher is done, the pitching coach can do one to two sets of pick-ups totaling 25 in each, with the pitching coach rolling the ball from left to right and right to left. The pitcher should be in a semi-squat position and without lifting his buttocks to maximize the use of his legs. It also creates a time of bonding with the pitcher showing him that you as a pitching coach care about his development.

NOTE: This program should be done the day after he pitches in a game. We want to minimize the long toss throws on the days he pitches in a game. Many pitchers do a lot of long toss throws before they pitch in a game and exerting that type of energy on noncompetitive throws with an uphill release point can be detrimental to his command on the mound when competing. A pitcher throwing with an uphill release point as he's warming up for a game should raise a red flag. It would be hard to expect him to get pitches at the bottom of the zone with ease, 15 minutes after he's done that type of throwing, and to get hitters out in quality locations. * **See figures 4-4 to 4-7**

64

Figure 4-4

Figure 4-5

FUNGO DRILL

THE PITCHER REINFORCES HIS DELIVERY AND RELEASE POINT IN THIS TYPE OF LONG TOSS PROGRAM

EYES ARE ON THE TARGET HE'S TRYING TO HIT

DOWN HILL PLANE ON HIS THROWS EASILY PUTS PITCHER ON TOP WITH HANDS & FINGERS BEHIND THE BASEBALL

Figure 4-6

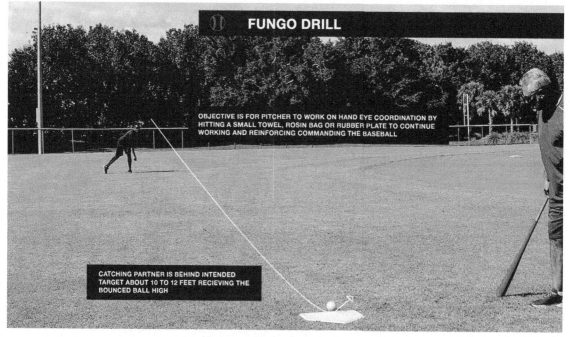

FUNGO DRILL

OBJECTIVE IS FOR PITCHER TO WORK ON HAND EYE COORDINATION BY HITTING A SMALL TOWEL, ROSIN BAG OR RUBBER PLATE TO CONTINUE WORKING AND REINFORCING COMMANDING THE BASEBALL

CATCHING PARTNER IS BEHIND INTENDED TARGET ABOUT 10 TO 12 FEET RECIEVING THE BOUNCED BALL HIGH

Figure 4-7

CHAPTER 5

Flat Ground Routine

A flat ground program is another vital daily aspect of pitching development.

All pitchers should have routines that they must do daily to prepare themselves for games. The flat ground program has a pitcher working at a 60% to 70% effort level for him to feel his mechanics, feel for pitches, use his hand-eye coordination, and still have enough in his tank for the game. Hand-eye coordination is our God-given talent to see a target and hit it with the baseball. When a pitcher takes the mound to compete, he should never think about mechanics unless he is so off with his command that he needs a personal time-out to figure things out. If something is not right during a game and it is affecting his control, he can grab the rosin bag and go over his mechanical checkpoints, but once he's back on the mound, it's all about hand-eye coordination. See the target and hit it or simply make a pitch by hitting the glove. This flat-ground throwing program should not exceed 20 to 25 pitches to work on your command and feel of one's pitches. A term you can use is locating fastball knee to knee. Use the left knee as the spot you're trying to hit, then do the same to the right knee hitting the glove every time. Have your partner put his glove on either knee. Ultimately the glove should be what the pitcher is focusing on before making a pitch.

Once the pitcher has gotten loose going out to maybe 90' or 120' feet or so, he comes back into 50' to 55'. He then gets his throwing partner down in the catcher's position, and he places his hat in front on the ground acting as a home plate and you as a pitcher can bring everything together.

We might not be pitching on this day, so it is imperative to make this as if it was your game. Our focus and concentration should be like an actual game to get the most out of this phase of our preparation. It's vital to work on your pre-pitch routine within this flat ground program. You should be in the zone because we as pitchers have a certain number of throws daily to prepare without losing our effectiveness for the games. We must take care of our arms and know where that number is daily. Pitchers like to throw, but in some cases, we as coaches must protect pitchers against themselves to be effective for games and prevent injuries.

Fastballs	4 to the left knee/ 4 to the right knee	All pitches for Strikes
Curve balls	3 middle down	With exception of put
Slider	3 middle down	away combinations
Change-up	3 middle down	
Put away Combinations	4 one off plate the other a strike	
Total:	21 Pitches	
	How many did I command?	
	Challenge Yourself	

The more command you have of your pitches daily, the more consistency you will achieve in games and the more confidence you will attain.

The Three C's

Concentration leads to consistency and consistency leads to confidence. You can't get confidence without the other two being in their proper place.

CHAPTER 6

Starters Pitch Routine (Using the Strings)

When a starting pitcher prepares for a game, he has a pitching routine he does to get him ready for competition. A pitch routine should make sense because preparation goes hand in hand with performance and results. The following are things a pitcher should consider when creating a bullpen pitch routine. One is how he uses his pitches in a game. Usually, a pitcher will throw around 60% percent fastballs, 25% between curveballs and sliders and lastly 15% percent changeups totaling 100 % of all pitches thrown.

We will use a 35-pitch bullpen routine as an example of how to go about structuring one, and it goes as follows. The first 30 pitches we will concentrate on throwing all strikes. Every pitch that comes out of your hand should be a strike during this stage of your routine. Major Leagues pitchers average a 63% strike to ball ratio in games and in this case, you will be working on 80% so that ratio can be easily reached. We finish this routine with two 2-pitch put away combinations. Many times, pitchers get to two strikes on hitters, and they do not have an idea on how to put hitters away.

Most pitchers do not practice put away combinations until they are in the game. With put-away combinations practiced, and then when faced with this situation in the game, the pitcher has rehearsed it to left-handed and right-handed hitters, and all we do is execute it and master it, to get hitters to chase pitches out of the zone in games. An example of a put-away combination from a right-handed pitcher to a right-handed hitter is a fastball in on the black to get him out followed by a slider an inch or two below the zone for a strikeout or an easy out. Another example is from a left-handed pitcher to a right-handed hitter: a change-up down and away, but one ball below the zone and a ball off the plate followed by a fastball on the black inside for a freeze strikeout or a jam shot broken bat type of result.

Since your fastball is your number one or most used pitch in competition, it should be the one we use most to get ready. We take seven fastballs and locate them to the glove or extension side, then the next seven to arm side. The objective is to see how many of each of those seven pitches we can locate to give us a close to accurate feel for where our command is on both sides of the plate.

Secondly, we throw our best command secondary pitch. We will throw four down the middle and more importantly down at the bottom of the zone. Getting this pitch over for strikes is vital to your success as a pitcher. A pitcher rarely has a chance to throw breaking balls out of the zone unless he has two strikes on the hitter. Throwing your breaking ball early for strikes will keep hitters from just sitting on your fastball and he will be more anxious to chase it out of the zone when he has two strikes.

Thirdly, your changeup is the most important pitch beside your fastball because it has the least average against pitch in the Major Leagues. When a pitcher has good arm speed simulating your fastball and doesn't slow down his body to help slow down the velocity of the pitch, hitters will have the toughest time to adjust to this pitch with everything being equal. Trusting the grip is the most critical piece to this puzzle because the pitcher can use his hand-eye God-given gift to throw this pitch for a strike. Pick up the glove and trust the grip only looking at a small spot inside the glove and try to hit it. Notice by how much you miss the glove, and then come back to get it exactly in the glove on the next pitch. We throw four right down the middle at the bottom of the zone for strikes. When a pitcher starts his bullpen routine, he should start from the stretch and finish from the wind-up. Why? Because unless he's a relief pitcher, making a spot start, he will always start from the windup, and secondly, most of our great pitches are made from the stretch in games. The catcher should always start down in a squat game like position. The pitcher is encouraged to throw five pitches from behind the back of the mound to reinforce shoulder and belt lines for angles as well as get over his front side to finish every pitch in games. The catcher should also be in front of the plate. Many times, a pitcher gets off to a slow start, and if he finishes his bullpen routine from the stretch and starts the game from the wind-up, it can take him some time to get into groove, rhythm, and tempo. Some pitchers are slow starters, and this is something I pay close attention to help the pitcher avoid having rough first innings.

The pitch routine on the chart shows how the pitch routine is broken down having each pitch with a purpose from beginning to end.

From the Stretch 1.3 and Under on Every Pitch		
Seven Fastballs Glove Side		7
Seven Fastballs Arm Side		7
	Total:	14
Four Change Ups Down Middle Down		4
Four CB's or Sliders Middle and Down		4
	Total:	22
From The Wind-Up		
Two Fastballs to Glove Side		2
Two Fastballs to Arm Side		2
	Total:	26
2 Change Ups Down Middle and Down		2
2 Curve Balls or Sliders Middle and Down		2
	Total:	30
Put Away Combinations		
1-2 Pitch Put away Combinations		2
1-2 Pitch Put away Combinations	Total:	2
1 Fastball Down the Middle and		1
Down		
	Total:	35

The pitcher is accountable for every pitch he makes in the game. Your bullpen routine will make you accountable for every pitch before it's time to compete which is a command measuring system. Your goal is to keep command and location as your number one priority.

Note: No two pitchers are the same and considering that this routine is a blueprint that can be tailored to your liking or your needs on any given day. If command of his secondary pitch isn't there, he can throw 4 or 5 extra pitches at the end of his bullpen session. He can take a couple of pitches off the fastball amount and incorporate it to the secondary pitch count. If his put away combinations are not where they should be, then throw one or two more combinations to be ready.

Figure 6-1

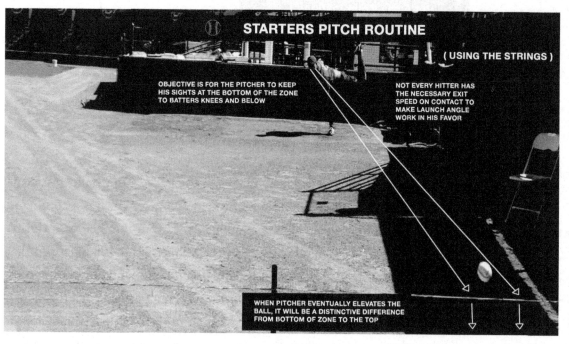

Figure 6-2

CHAPTER 7

Relievers Pitch Routine (Using the Strings)

Relief pitchers are a different breed than starting pitchers because they thrive on adrenaline and they are like doctors always on call. The relief pitcher has a role on a pitching staff that indicates when he's going to pitch in the game. The long man covers early innings or when a starter gets off to a bad start or is injured, the long man in the bullpen steps into the game. He specializes in keeping the game where it is to hand it to the specially designated pitchers who pitch to lefty-righty matchups or set up man, or closer to finish. Depending on their role on the bullpen staff, he will warm up accordingly with the outfielders during the game. If he's the long man, he will play catch early with the outfielders. If he's a middleman, he'll warm up during the middle innings, and if he's a set-up man or closer, he uses the later innings to get loose.

It is a pitcher's responsibility to get loose and stretch during a game and be prepared and ready to compete when his number is called to pitch.

1. A relief pitcher must keep the following things in mind. Will he be pitching from the wind up or from the stretch when he enters the game? If the pitcher pitches from the stretch, then will he go into the game with runners on bases or not.

2. If runners are on base, he will need to deliver the baseball in 1.3 seconds to the plate. Why? Because the average base runner gets to 2nd base in 3.3 seconds and between the pitcher and catcher, we must equal that time to have a chance get them out.

3. We must get loose quickly unless instructed otherwise by your coach. A relief pitcher should be paying close attention to the game to get a feel for when he will pitch. That is why we throw with outfielders so, when you get the call, it won't take long to get ready.

4. Know which batters you will be facing and once loose, work on the pitches you will need to execute in the game and practice them. Command is always your priority

5. Avoid throwing a game in the bullpen. Meaning once you are ready to go, match the pitcher in game pitch to pitch. When he makes two, you make one or just wait, remembering you have eight on game mound.

6. Focus, focus, focus.

7. Visualization is a vital part of your preparation. Visualize yourself making each pitch in your mind, so when the time comes in the game, you have already made them.

This table is an example of a Relief pitchers pitch routine. You can tailor yours to your comfort. Good pitchers have solid routines, and you are no different as you embark on your journey to greatness.

From the Stretch 1.3 and Under on Every Pitch		
6 to 8 pitches to get loose		6-8
4 FBs Glove Side and Down		4
4 FBs Arm Side and Down		4
	Total:	8
3 SLs or CBs Middle		3
3 CHs Middle		3
	Total:	14
2 1-2 Pitch Put Away Combinations		4
	Total:	18
Total (including pitches to get loose)		24-26

CHAPTER 8

Pre-Pitch Routine

A pre-pitch routine is a vital part of pitchers in game standard. It allows the pitcher to flow with his rhythm and tempo. A study done on a hitter's ability to adjust from pitch to pitch is approximately 13 seconds. We strive to make pitches in 12 seconds to make hitters uncomfortable and not give them time to get set mentally and physically. This time gets altered if there is a foul ball because, by the time you get a new ball or possibly a ball boy replenishing baseballs to the umpire, time has elapsed.

A good tempo is what keeps the game moving efficiently and keeps your defense on their toes ready to make plays behind you. There are many benefits to having the game move quickly.

What is a pre-pitch routine? A pre-pitch routine is a systematic synchronized and coordinated action a pitcher does between each pitch. If you were to ask pitchers to look at the dirt on the mound, and then ask them what they see? They will say they see dirt 99% of the time. What you do next is ask them if they can look and see the texture of the dirt. Ask them to pick a small pebble and focus on that pebble. *See figure 8-1

His focus and concentration automatically goes to another level. Next ask them to look at the grass in front of the mound and what do they see? The answer should again be grass. *See figure 8-2

Next, ask them to find and focus on a blade of grass not the sea of grass. *See figure 8-3

Have them track their vision to the feet of the catcher and up to the fingers giving signs. *See figure 8-4

Next, have them work on picking up the glove and look at a small piece of the inside of that glove to take their focus to the highest level to make a pitch. *See figure 8-5

This focus and concentration routine can be used to challenge yourself as a pitcher to have on every single pitch. This routine has an added component, and that is when runners reach base.

Situational pitching creates a way for a pitcher to be challenged in his focus and concentration. Once a situation presents itself, we as pitchers need to have a mental routine that we go to stay cool, calm, and collected during the pressure situations a game will present to us. At this point, a pitcher can use the grass as the place where he evaluates the situation.

He then gets on the dirt to go over which pitches he will need to get the results he wants. Next, he gets on the rubber and thinks about nothing other than executing each pitch that will give him the result he just planned out one at a time, keeping command his priority. *See figure 8-6

Distractions are a big part of the game that pitchers learn to deal with, and this system gives you the ability to stay focused on every single pitch when competing in the game.

To put this system into play, a pitcher steps on the mound and possibly wipes the dirt from the front of the rubber with his spikes. The pitcher then starts the process of picking up the dirt, the blades of the grass, followed by the catcher's fingers then the small part of the mitt and hits that spot with his pitch. From the stretch, he gets into his position and looks straight down and begins the same process. When the game speeds up, a pitcher can slow the process down by thinking of the game situation on the grass. Then he gets on the dirt of the mound and thinks about the combination of pitches that will give him the desired result. Its time to get on the rubber and execute the command of his pitches. This system will allow you to clear your mind of anything except on making the pitch and allowing you to keep your focus on the task at hand.

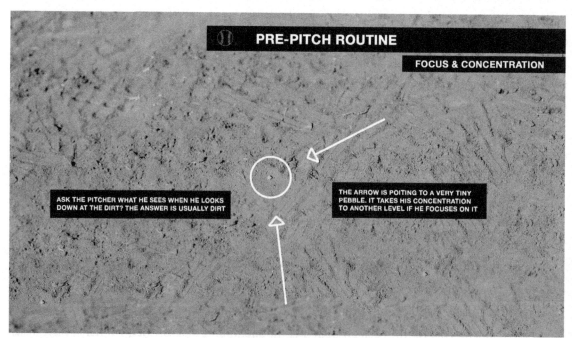

Figure 8-1

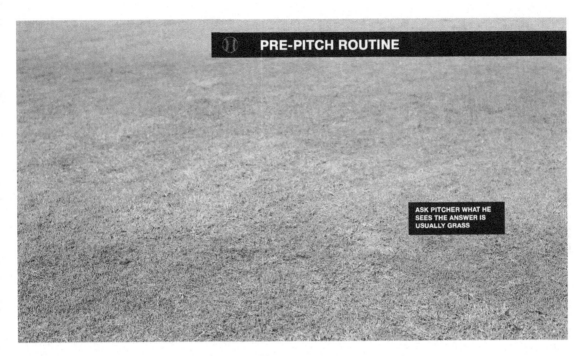

Figure 8-2

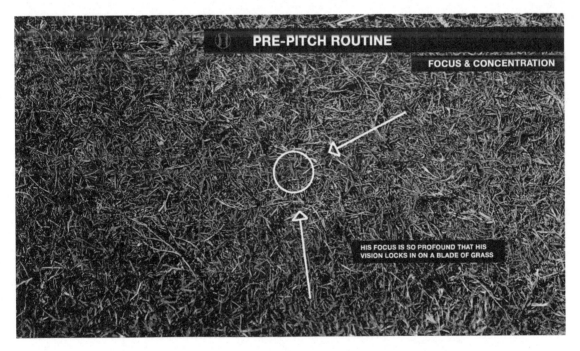

Figure 8-3

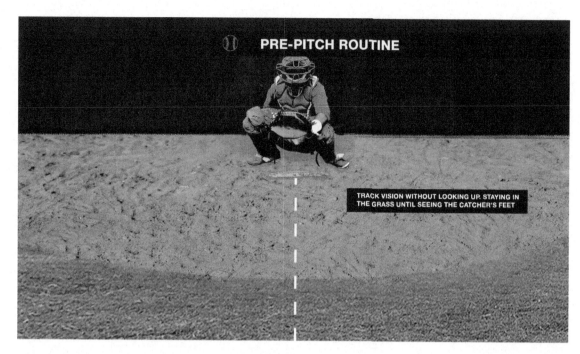

Figure 8-4

Figure 8-5

Figure 8-6

CHAPTER 9

Pitches and Grips

Pitches and grips vary from pitcher to pitcher and coach to coach. We all come in different shapes, sizes, and colors. Some of us are tall, some short, some with big hands and long fingers, and some with small hands and short fingers. When it comes to grips, our finger sensors coupled with hand size determine which grip best suites us. As a former pitcher and now a coach for over 21 years, I will share which grips on different pitches work best for me as well as the pitchers I have worked with and developed over the years. Experimenting with different grips usually happens when pitchers are simply playing catch with each other. One of the pitchers sees another pitcher that throws an above-average slider for example and goes over to ask, how he grips and throws that pitch. It's the ultimate compliment a pitcher can get who throws a special pitch.

On the other hand, pitchers themselves are curious and experiment with a different grip and a new pitch can evolve and create new life. I call this phase of a pitcher's program the playpen because it's the place while playing catch and having fun with your teammates can launch a career-changing experience which can result in a scholarship, being drafted, being called to the big leagues, or making it to the Hall of Fame.

Four Seam Fastball

We will first dive in with the fastball. Many pitchers today are drawn to the cutter because of its late movement for a fastball. In this introduction, we will start with the conventional four-seam grip. When gripping a four-seamer, I recommend turning the half-circle part of the horseshoe towards your ring finger whether you are a righthanded or a lefthanded pitcher. Since your middle finger is the longest one on your hand, it should be placed on the widest part of the horseshoe and your pointing finger should be placed where the seams start to get narrower on the ball for a perfect fit. The thumb should be on the bottom seam right under the knuckles of your hand creating a triangle between your pointing and middle finger. There should be plenty of space between the ball and the back part of your thumb to avoid choking the ball. The objective is to create as much backspin on the baseball as you drive your fingers through the ball at release. Some pitchers create such great spin rate that even if the velocity isn't high, the backspin creates a high rate of swings and misses. * **See figure 9-1**

Two-Seam Fastball

In today's world of cutters and four-seam fastballs, the two-seamer also referred to as a sinker, has somewhat lost the luster it once had. The hitter's emergence of launch angle and trying to get under pitches to create loft on balls put in play has the pitching industry locating pitches more at the top of the strike zone to counter this approach. It has created more four-seamers at the top of the strike zone and cutters to get above or off the sweet spot of the bat. Nevertheless, the two-seam fastball has a place in the game to counter these angles hitters are trying to create, when a ground ball is needed for a double play or if the infield is in with a runner on third base and less than two outs. Different grips work for different pitchers, but the one I have found to have the best results is placing both power fingers (pointing and middle fingers) inside the narrow seams. The thumb is placed on the first cross seam under the ball to create space and to prevent choking the ball. Because you've placed your thumb on that first cross seam, your middle and pointing fingers should be on the smooth part of the ball, just in front of the narrow seams. The narrow seams act as a track or rail for your fingers to be inside and alongside them. There should be little to no space between your fingers. Most pitchers throw a two-seamer off the pads of their fingertips. With this release, we must drive the tips of our nails through the front of the ball to maximize pronation of the arm leading to great extension through the pitch. The results I've encountered is that the sink occurs very late, breaking two planes as hitters start to swing at the height he sees, but makes contact on the second break or plane of the pitch, inducing a ground ball, a foul ball or a swing and miss. ***See figure 9-2**

Slider

The slider is a pitch like a sinker when thrown correctly, they break late, making the hitter see fastball out of your hand, but as it nears the plate, it goes to a lower plane at around 8 to 10 miles slower. When the hitter initiates his swing for a fastball, the pitch breaks late to the lower plane below the bat, causing the hitter to be out front with a swing, or miss the pitch altogether. The most successful grip I teach is placing your middle finger on the wide part of the horseshoe that starts to curve just under the Rawlings logo. If you're left-handed, the middle finger is just below "lings" of the Rawlings' logo, and if you're a right-handed pitcher, it is just below the "Raw" of the same logo. The thumb should be placed on the bottom horseshoe seam for counter-presser. When squeezing the thumb with light pressure into the seam, one should feel that middle finger applying pressure on the front part of the ball. When releasing the slider, the pitcher should feel and think that he's releasing with the middle finger in front of the ball to create a maximum spin that leads to a tight, late break. The spin should create a red dot in the middle of the ball as it nears the plate. It is essential that a pitcher follows through after release to maximize late break on the pitch. Keep in mind that the slider is usually easier to teach and throw for strikes over the curveball, so if a pitcher is having difficulty throwing a curveball, the natural course of action is to teach the pitcher to throw a slider for strikes which will allow him to compete in games. * **See figure 9-3**

Curveball

The curveball is a great pitch because it usually is 12 to 14 miles slower than your fastball and has 12 to 6 or 11 to 5 breaking action from a right-handed pitcher and vice versa from a left-hander. The few pitchers that throw good curveballs offset hitters' timing because we as humans see things moving laterally easier than up and down. When a hitter sees the curveball at its apex, the ball starts to come down at a fast rate of rotation, which makes it extremely difficult for the eyes to track and follow a disappearing ball towards the ground. When the curveball is thrown correctly, it has a very tight spin for the break, speed, and depth to be efficient and be a viable weapon in a pitcher's arsenal. The grip I recommend is pitched with four seams to maximize downward rotation on a vertical axis. The pitcher can place his middle finger along the seam just before the wide part of the horseshoe is about to turn and the thumb on the bottom seam where the seam is doing the same turn. The ball can be choked with little to no space on the web of the hand. The key to throwing a good curveball for a strike is where one starts or releases it. There are two ways to approach this technique. A pitcher can release it by thinking to start it at the catcher's mask. The other school of thought is throwing it to the glove. If the pitcher starts it at the mask, the pitcher will have to take into consideration how much his curveball breaks for a strike to determine where it is to be started. The pitcher should throw it for a strike at the hitters' knees, or the bottom of the strike zone. The pitcher who concentrates on hitting the glove can make the adjustment by how far he misses the glove. For example, if the curveball passes the glove, he's releasing too out front, and if the curveball misses on the arm side of the glove, he's releasing it too far back. By gaging the misses, one can find the happy medium to hit the glove for a strike all the while maintaining his eyes on the catcher's mitt. To expand the zone for a strikeout, the pitcher must start the curveball in the strike zone making it look like a strike but ends up being a ball for a possible swing and miss. A pitcher also has an option of starting the curveball to opposite side hitter with two strikes for a ball but catching the corner for a strike. That curveball is called a back door. The curveballs that bounce on the back of home plate gives hitters fits as that pitch stays in the strike zone for an extended period before descending to the ground. * **See figure 9-4**

Changeup

The changeup as mentioned before is the pitch with the least average against at the Major League Level. Pitchers that throw changeups without slowing the body down, or over manipulate the ball to make it move or change release points, give hitters a difficult time when it comes to recognition. The changeup is the pitch that most resembles a fastball based on backspin and release, with everything being equal in the pitcher's body and release out of hand. The great thing about the changeup when thrown correctly, the pitch approaches the plate at 10 to 14 miles off your fastball. Most good changeups have a downward arm side sinking or fading action. The hitters swing at arm speed versus velocity of the pitch. Many Major League starters have had successful careers throwing fastballs and changeups with an average to just below average third pitch, which is a reason many experienced pitchers, wonder why it took them so long to be convinced on learning the changeup earlier in their careers. The grip I favor with a changeup is a four-seam grip.

The middle finger is placed alongside the curve of the wide part of the horseshoe, and the pressure is mostly focused on that finger and seam. The ring finger is placed just on the outside of the apex of the ball. The pinky and pointing finger should be pressed or feeling as they are pinching the sides of the ball. The thumb should be placed on the seam directly under the middle finger. Two recommendations are to remind the pitcher throwing this changeup to apply pressure with the thumb and feel how the middle and ring fingers counter that pressure, all the while keeping a loose wrist to maximize a whip-like action through release. With this 4-seam grip, we focus on getting the pad and tip of the finger to drive through the front of the ball to create maximum backspin. A pitcher can throw his changeup to both arm side and opposite side hitters to avoid them from eliminating a pitch from your repertoire. We often hear coaches say to a pitcher to trust the grip and let it rip. Well, my definition to that is for the pitcher to take his mind completely off the grip because the grip will give you the contrast in velocity and movement, but the eyes and hand will give you the command. What we as pitchers learn to do is use the hand-eye coordination to let your eyes tell the hand and fingers where to throw the pitch. If the pitcher misses the glove, make the adjustment with the eyes and the hand which is what pitchers do with the fastball -- trust the grip and let it rip.

If a pitcher throws a two-seam fastball, then he should complement it with a two-seam change-up which is illustrated on the second picture on the right-hand side. With the 2-seam grip, one tries to get fingers in front of the narrow seams and the thumb on the first bottom cross seam. We like to remind pitchers to try to get pads of middle and ring fingers along the wider part of the horseshoe getting off the apex of the ball. It will make it easy to release and feel the inside of the ball to maximize the fading action movement.

In closing, the bread and butter and lifeline of a pitcher is his ability to get hitters out with command of his repertoire. Two things get hitters out, and that is location and speed of the pitch. As we mentioned earlier, fastball command is at the top of the list. The ability to change speeds with your secondary pitches is number two. Reading and recognizing the point of contact is three. The developed mental toughness, of clearing your mind with nothing other than hitting the glove, is number four. And finally, having conviction and complete confidence on the pitch the pitcher is about to make rounds out my number five. When pitchers have the command and movement, it leads to the three "C's. Again, the three "C's" are concentration, that leads to consistency, which ultimately leads to confidence. When having these five things in order, all a pitcher needs is a game plan to execute. * **See figure 9-5**

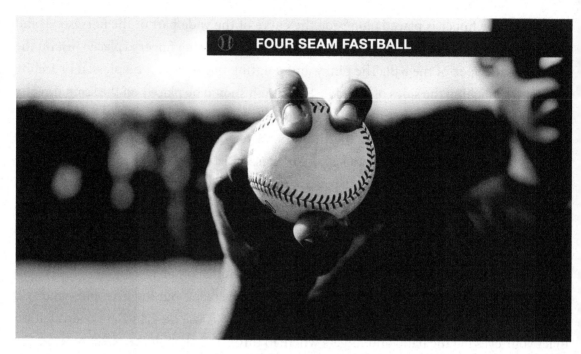

FOUR SEAM FASTBALL

Figure 9-1

TWO SEAM FASTBALL

Figure 9-2

Figure 9-3

Figure 9-4

Figure 9-5

CHAPTER 10

Cat and Mouse Game-Countering Hitting Approaches

The cat and mouse game between pitcher and hitter

To become a complete pitcher, one must be dedicated in all facets of pitching. All the small things are each big to a winning pitcher. Once a pitcher learns how to control the baseball and throw it over the plate, we need to develop the ability to command the ball in the nine regions of the strike zone. We should go over the opposing team's lineup to see which hitters you should get out, the hitters who give you difficulty, and the hitters you will not allow to beat you in a crucial game situation as you develop the game plan. A pitcher needs to know the DNA of all hitters in the opposing lineup. Which hitters get on base by walking a lot and which ones strike out a good portion of the time. The pitcher gauges discipline versus free swingers. A pitcher should also anticipate having two tough or rough innings, so he is mentally prepared and focused when they arise to make the game swaying pitches.

Too many pitchers consume themselves on not allowing solid contacts. We tend to give hitters so much respect or credit that we back ourselves into a corner with few options, as opposed to exposing their vulnerabilities. A hitter's vulnerability is looking for their pitch to hit. Most pitchers do not take advantage of this, instead of being aggressive in the strike zone. The first question we should ask ourselves is where is their pitch? Usually, their pitch is a little more than middle of the plate and in, early in the count. The more the count is in their favor 1-0, 2-0, 3-0, 2-1, 3-1, the more they can cheat to get to that zone, enhancing the probabilities of squaring that pitch and hitting it solid.

Some hitters call this being in Beast Mode or Hunting fastballs. As a pitcher, we should think of it as a seventeen-inch plate becoming smaller with every ball you throw. For example, envision the plate going from seventeen inches to ten to eight to seven inches shrinking with every ball one throws. Hitting the other way goes against a hitter's DNA for the most part. The game has changed today regarding defending or run prevention at the Major League level, with teams putting their infielders in what is called the shift alignment. The shift was predominantly used against left-handed hitters, but now it's also used on right-handed hitters as well. To the left-handed hitters, they put the third baseman where the shortstop normally plays, shortstop now is on the right side of second base and the second baseman is more to the pull-side and on the outfield grass -- basically bunching up the right side of the infield due to many hitters consistently hitting specifically to that part of the field. Some of these hitters are reduced to bunting the ball down the third base side to get a hit. The hitters are challenged to hit the ball the other way, and they still have tremendous difficulties doing it. One of the first, if not the first hitter in baseball to have the shift applied to, was Ted Williams. He was one of the best hitters of all time and the last hitter to hit .400. When they shifted the defense on him, he had the most challenging time hitting in his career, so it stands to reason if it was difficult to hit the other way for Ted Williams, you can imagine how difficult it is for the rest. Pitching on the L, which is the bottom of the zone to both left-handed or right-hand hitters and vertical on the inner part of the plate is the start. This L has been around for as long as pitchers have toed the rubber, yet pitching programs fail to break down this simple system on how much easier it can be to get hitters out.

When we understand where the hitters' kryptonite lies, it starts to put our preparation into perspective. What is the number one ability I must master to be successful? The answer is fastball command on the L. The L is an imaginary line on the plate that goes from the height of the batter's knees to the outside part of the plate and vertically up to the top of the strike zone on the inner half of each hitter. The next question is why? Because hitters are looking for their pitch to hit early in an at-bat and if we try to be too fine, they feel it will lead to us falling behind in the count, making it much easier for them to hit. This situation is called zone hitting. If the pitch isn't in that zone, hitting coaches teach hitters to lay off that pitch early in order not to get themselves out, or until they are forced into swinging at that location and that is in a two-strike situation. It is what the industry teaches hitters to increase their O.B.P.% (On Base Percentage). Picture the seventeen-inch plate becoming a 25-inch plate or so, making hitters susceptible to swinging at pitches outside of the strike zone. Our number one pitch is the fastball, and by commanding it, we put them in SWING MODE, consequently taking us to our second ability--which are our secondary pitches--to get hitters out front of the fastball speed, that we have commanded and established. What is SWING MODE? The definition of swing mode is when a pitcher has forced the hitter into swinging the bat due to the command of his fastball in and out in the strike zone. The hitter will need to be aggressive early to not get into a position where he is looking for too many spots in the strike zone with two strikes making it extremely difficult to hit for success.

We will make them start to think, and that's when we begin to have the upper hand on the hitter. The reason hitters start to think in two-strike situations is that it takes seven balls to cover the 17 inches of the plate, which is one side to the other. It takes another nine balls to cover the height of the strike zone, which means we have forced them into looking for 63 baseballs to hit in the strike zone if you multiply 9x7 you get 63. On the other hand, when hitters are in early or ahead counts, they can now look for six balls, but the balls are on top of each other three on top and three on the bottom, not spread individually across the plate (Called Zone hitting). Take notice of what your curveball, change-up, slider, etc. are called secondary pitches. The Fastball is your primary pitch, Number one, Número Uno.

Pitching inside with your fastball is the next important ability we must develop to make your fastball look like 2 or 3 different pitches. We need to keep in mind that defensive coaches swing their outfielders towards the opposite field when opposing hitters have two strikes for the most part. They also have them position themselves deeper and more to pull-side when they are ahead in counts. Why? Because they are aware that hitters are just surviving or in the SCRAMBLING mode when they have two strikes looking middle away and are just reduced to protecting on inside fastballs. Hitters are thought to widen their stance, shorten their swing, and choke up on the bat. Why? If we locate our fastball on the inner part of the L, we add about 3 miles an hour to our fastball by forcing the hitter to make contact out front leading to velocity efficiency or perceived velocity.

We decide what part of the field the batter will hit the ball due to commanding that fastball. When hitters must be concerned with the fastball in those two locations, out and in, or in and out, they have difficulties. When we make mistakes out and over the plate, not only with our fastball, but also with secondary pitches, it is because the pitcher has the hitter so engaged on location that if the pitcher makes a mistake up, and middle of the plate, they are caught by surprise or just not ready for it. Hitters take advantage of those mistakes when a pitcher lacks command and makes them more often.

The New York Yankees thrived on pitchers nibbling to get into good hitting counts. Three, four, and five starters in the big leagues do not attack the strike zone as well as the number one and two pitchers of a rotation. The Yankees took the on-base percentage approach.

Their approach was to take pitches and try and get into hitters' counts to make solid contact as well to get the starter out of a game as early as possible and see if they can make the opposing staff make 160 total pitches in that game. That usually meant they beat up that pitching staff for that game. That approach works during the season, but usually not during the playoffs. Why? Because in the playoffs you will be facing the one-two- and three starters of a rotation in a five or seven-game series and they attack the strike zone with good fastball command better than four and five starters. We should train our minds like we train our bodies. Baseball is a hand-eye coordination sport, and at times we worry so much about mechanics that we lose sight of what the act of pitching is all about. Pitching isn't just about first-pitch strikes or inducing contact on three pitches or less or inducing more ground balls than fly balls. It's also understanding what hitters' approaches are, and what they are trying to do, and combining that with good command of your good pitches, which usually leads to the old cliché that good pitching beats good hitting. When a pitcher locates his fastball down and away to the outer part of the strike zone consistently, he accomplishes many things. The first action the pitcher witnesses is that hitters usually take that pitch down and away if executed precisely early in the count.

1. If a hitter makes contact, he usually hits it foul due to the pitcher forcing the hitter to have a diagonal bat angle and hands, barrel, and ball are at three different places. This makes it extremely hard to make consistent solid contact and hitting it deep in the strike zone is the hardest to gauge for hitters who a pitcher has forced into going the other way.

2. Undisciplined hitters who swing at that location early, have a hard time allowing the baseball to travel deeper in the zone, consequently hitting it in front and rolling over to the shortstop or second baseman, and if in the air, infielders trot back for a lazy fly ball or outfielders come running in on a soft easy fly ball out.

3. Locating this pitch down and away leads to what all pitchers love - First pitch outs.

If pitchers miss a ball or two up or more over the white of the plate, then we as pitchers need to be aware and take responsibility for missing our intended target and solid contact has a high probability of happening. The pitcher has allowed the batter to now have his hands, barrel, and ball to be on the same plane, which can result in solid contact. Keeping the barrel diagonally as many times as possible should be one of the biggest goals for a pitcher. The game also changes the thoughts and aggressiveness of the hitters. The deeper the game gets and the more you have established command of your fastball down and away for strikes they get into a subconscious panic mode. They panic about what? They panic on not getting into a two-strike situation because numbers do not lie, and all hitters know batting averages are significantly and dramatically lower causing self-imposed internal pressure that ultimately leads to uncharacteristic swings.

Hitting coaches teach their hitters with two strikes that most pitches are going to be down and away so, they should look for the pitches they will see on that side of the plate. They learn to fight off the inside pitch and hit the ones away solid. This brings us to the two-strike approach. I've witnessed more than one hitting coach teach their hitters that if a pitcher throws them a two-strike fastball on the black, to tip their hats off to them and get them next time. Why this advice? Because most pitchers pitch away with two strikes, so they ask hitters to spread their feet, to shorten up their swing, possibly choke up on the bat for bat control. Hit it hard somewhere and make the defense make a play to get the hitter out. I've heard hitting coaches say to hitters to play glorified pepper which means swing short and quick and put it in play. A very important piece of information and advice I can share with you based on my experience and years in coaching is that when you locate your fastball on the black or edge of the plate, the hitter has difficulties distinguishing if it's going to be a ball or a strike. Visually there's a fine line that freezes his reaction. Hitters are taught to stay inside the baseball, and a pitcher that can shave the black part of the plate with his fastball will convolute his visual message and confuse the signal path to the hands to swing the bat. This will cause a freezing or late reaction to get the barrel to the ball because he cannot tell if it's a ball or a strike.

For pitchers to maintain the use of fastballs on both parts of the plate the first time through a line-up, a pitcher-catcher combination can use multiple headshakes, as it is in place to plant a seed in hitters mind. Even though hitters have a plan, the multiple headshakes can put a thought in his mind of a secondary pitch, and that's what we're looking for, to continue to throw the fastball. Pitchers should use two of the pitches in his repertoire if he can as he's pitching the first time through the order to have another pitch when he faces hitters the second time up. Unless a pitcher gets into an early jam, he does not need to show hitters his complete repertoire the first time he goes through the line-up.

Once a pitcher has established that fastball away early and inside late in the count, we can then start to change the sequences second or third time through the batting order like an 0-0 fastball inside, or a 0-1 fastball inside after conditioning the hitter to look for that location away consistently early in counts the first time through the order. If a hitter wants to ambush a pitcher, then we can throw a first-pitch curveball, slider or change-up for a strike to keep the hitter guessing, or get him off balance, as well as stay one step ahead of him to throw off his timing. Ambush means that a hitter is coming up to the plate cheating on the fastball and has put all his eggs in one basket and is going to jump all over on the first pitch he sees, which should be a fastball in his mind middle in of the plate. If a pitcher pays attention to hitters, he will know who these hitters are that like to ambush. Remember that a hitter can cheat all he wants, but the location of the pitch usually determines his success to square a pitch. There is no such thing as a GET ME OVER Curveball or Slider.

On the other hand, there is a Curveball or Slider for a strike. Get me over Curveballs or Sliders can be hit a long way due to them becoming cement mixtures that stay up and in the zone without break or depth and are 10 to 14 mph slower than the fastball. The reason it's hard to hit a good Curveball or Slider is that the eyes were not meant to see well up and down. They were meant to see straight and laterally. That is the reason they can hit a Curveball or Slider that stays on that horizontal plane well. The Curveball or Slider are pitches we need to not only throw for a strike at the bottom of the zone but also backdoor it, where good hitters give up on it out of your hand because it looks like a ball but as it nears the plate, it catches the outside corner for a freeze strikeout. This curveball or sliders are preferably thrown to buy a strike or with two strikes to freeze the hitter. The other location is called the wrap or back foot curveball or slider where it bores in on the opposite side hitter, out of the strike zone for a strikeout. That one is called the wipeout pitch.

Lastly, the bounced curveball or slider on the back part of the plate is one of the most challenging pitches that hitters have trouble laying off because it looks like a strike until the last possible second and it breaks beneath the zone. Keep in mind that most hitters bat from the back part of the batter's box specifically on the backline of the batter's box, so that bounced curveball or slider is still in front of their stance making it virtually impossible to hit once they've committed to swing at it. Hitting is timing, and we as pitchers develop the ability to throw off that timing by commanding the baseball and using our secondary pitches. The changeup is a great pitch to have in our repertoire. During a game as the pitcher goes through the course of his pitch-to-pitch journey, hitters at some point will time your fastball. The changeup is a great pitch to throw that timing off and stay one step ahead of him. We can use it to get a hitter off your fastball. We can use it on a dead pull hitter early or late in an at-bat. We can use it with a one-second hold slide step, change up to throw both runner and batter off, and create a bad jump at 1st base, and a batter lunging to jump on the fastball because of your quick pitch delivery, but slow pitch combination inducing a possible double play ball. The changeup can be a great weapon to have in your repertoire, and it's another pitch that will be of concern to the hitter.

The way to make a hitter start to think is by filling up the spots in the strike zone. He's allowing you to fill up and once you show him you can fill those spots up; he will start to panic and get out of his game which is the time we will see uncharacteristic swings and approaches.

Adrian Gonzales said while being a guest speaker to the Los Angeles Dodgers minor leaguers, that he doesn't worry when a pitcher is throwing 95 to 98 mph and missing up in the zone. He can catch up to that velocity with poor location. On the other hand, if a pitcher is 88-91 mph, but can locate it in and out, up and down, and back and forth it will keep him guessing and off balance with timing. He also mentioned, "No one can hit that fastball down and away at the knees, not even Barry Bonds." If you look at Adrian's numbers stated by him, he's good middle away, and middle away and up, but down and away is extremely difficult for him to hit with any authority. When a pitcher can locate his fastball down and away, he has controlled the batters bat angle, which is the reason hitters have so many difficulties making solid contact.

On the other hand, if the pitcher elevates his fastball, the pitcher loses the battle of controlling the bat angle, which is vital for controlling contact. It doesn't matter what the situation is. The money pitch is down and away!!! Keep in mind the pitch down and away puts hands, barrel of the bat, and ball in three different places as I mentioned before. A diagonal bat angle is hard to square or center a ball up. I cannot emphasize the diagonal bat angle point enough.

We as pitchers are in the business of taking away at-bats. Their coaches teach them not to give at-bats away. When we strike on the L, we are in the process of taking at-bats away from hitters. When pitchers get behind in counts, hitters begin to hunt fastballs, and if those fastballs are up and over the middle of the plate, they usually get hammered.

Once the pitcher has established the ability to dot or located the fastball on the L, he should be able to see or recognize when hitters start to cheat either by trying to dive over the plate to get to that outside pitch or open up the front side anticipating that inside pitch. Pitchers need to be one step ahead of hitters by changing location once they tip or you recognize something different in their stance or swings. Keep in mind that good hitters are successful 30% of the time or get three hits in 10 at-bats. When we master this approach, we take this percentage down to 25% or so. We will be pitching on the edges, but not nibbling which is a big difference. Nibblers avoid contact as appose to L pitchers who embrace contact, but more importantly putting pressure on hitters having 0-1 or 0-2 counts consistently. Take notice why the games great pitchers get hitters out so easily from Roy Halladay, Pedro Martinez, Jacob deGrom to Clayton Kershaw and Jon Lester. Hitters in the big leagues know they better jump on the first good fastball they see, if not, it's an

0-2 situation and is pretty much at the mercy and hands of these great pitchers. These great pitchers know and thrive on the fastball command.

Hitters today are taught to have better launch angles to produce more home runs. We are starting to see how vulnerable they are to the high chest fastball combined with the bottom to below the bottom of the strike zone curveball. This pitch combination is producing a high rate of swings and misses at the MLB level.

What we have done in this chapter is to give pitchers ideas of what to be aware of when putting together a game plan. I am not telling you to throw anything but fastballs, just understand how necessary the command of your fastball is to your success and how difficult pitching can become without having this ability. I have seen firsthand the pitchers on my pitching staff who did not understand this simple principle and have been weeded out of professional baseball early in their careers. The pitchers with staying power recognize that hitters thrive on mistakes left up on the middle of the plate. They do everything required to develop their fastball command. It is evident that pitchers need to throw their secondary pitches early in counts to keep them thinking and off balance. To get hitters out, pitchers sometimes should pitch backward early in a game or, in other words, throw curveballs, sliders, or change-ups first to set up their fastball. But even if you pitch backward, a pitcher must be able to locate that fastball because if hitters eliminate it from your repertoire, a pitcher could be in for a long night or early exit. There are good fastball-hitting teams, and a pitcher needs to be able to adjust to whatever he's confronted with, but it all will eventually come back to fastball command.

CHAPTER 11

The Art of Throwing Off Hitters Timing

Hitting is timing and pitchers are supposed to throw off that timing. A pitcher must change speeds with secondary pitches such as a curveball, slider, or change-up to throw that timing off once a pitcher has established his fastball command. When I pitched and then started to coach, I saw pitching mainly from the view of the pitcher's mound. Being in the dugout with former catchers Pat Borders, Gary Carter, and Razor Shines, I started to see the game from a whole new side and perspective, and that was from a catcher's eyes, through the mask, and out to the pitcher's mound. I learned to see things I couldn't see before that brought my attention and awareness to a whole new level. Lengthy conversations and stationed in the trenches during games have led me to this vital information. I learned to anticipate what a hitter is thinking and what he needs to do to be comfortable with his rhythm and timing to hit on his terms. The technique I will share with you has nothing to do with pitches and everything to do with timing. One of the hitting instructors I worked along-side with talked about having the foot down early for the hitter to recognize pitches and have enough time to start his swing and square the ball up with consistency. If the hitter's front foot was down too late, the hitter will be at a distinct disadvantage with little to no time to react and hit a pitched ball traveling 90 or more miles an hour when it crosses the hitting zone.

This coach talked about breaking down the video in terms of timing between the pitchers' release point to when the ball crosses the hitting zone. The idea was to have hitters land and have their stride foot down on 5 to 6 clicks of the 12 clicks it takes for the ball to travel from the pitcher's fingertips to the hitting zone. When the ball leaves the pitcher's hand, every click is equivalent to four feet as it nears the plate. When slowing it down frame by frame, it gives hitters an exact time he should have his stride foot down based on clicks. Once again, the 5 to 6 clicks on the video break down, is when they want to land to hit comfortably, which is the magic word associated with timing. Everything they do in drills is based on a three-count, which covers the pitcher's load, hand separation, and release point, during tee-work, flips, and regular batting practice.

In *Unleash the Pitcher in You*, we've already covered pitching within 12 seconds of previous pitch coupled with a 3-step drop. The 3-step drop means once making a pitch and your follow-through foot hits the ground, the pitcher takes that same foot and proceeds to walk backward allowing you the timing to catch the ball from the catcher on the rubber as you've completed your third step. This keeps you working at a fast pace causing intentional and subconscious anxiety in hitters because their internal clock needs at least 13 seconds to readjust to the next pitch. If we keep hitters timing at that frantic pace, we affect their homeostasis, which stems from the hypothalamus part of the brain. The pitcher wants to force the hitter to get time from the umpire to get his mind and body synchronization back in order.

When Pat Borders was a catcher in the Major Leagues, he gained his experience on pitch calling and sequencing pitches. This experience came during one of the more difficult times when hitters were the toughest to get out. It was during the performance enhancement era. As we all know, many hitting records were broken when it came to home runs. He needed to learn how to be creative because pitchers Earned Run Averages were on the rise. He instinctively learned that to have success one had to tap into the timing of hitters, especially when they were in hitting counts, which is also referred to hunting fastball, or being in beast mode. Establishing the 12 seconds between pitches, the pitcher puts the hitter in a fast count of timing and Pat learned to apply the complete opposite when in hitting counts. The idea was to make pitches, but with a longer or delayed count. The objective was to get hitters past their comfort timing zone and make them wait until a thought had entered their mind, taking hitters away from the focused thinking of see the ball, hit the ball. Based on his hitting body gestures, a pitcher will see the cue when to make the pitch. It's getting the hitter to the brink of calling time out and making the pitch. If the hitter calls time out and gets it from the umpire, then a pitcher needs to quick-pitch the hitter when he's stepping back into the batter's box, which adversely is the opposite of making him wait. Once the hitter steps back into the batter's box and is ready to hit, the pitcher quick pitches him, but under control being careful he doesn't throw off his timing, and rushes, consequently missing on a very important pitch. After being part of this system and seeing it in games, I have witnessed countless swings and misses or easy soft contact outs either by slowing down the hitter's pace or quick-pitching him as it stopped the opposing team's momentum or shifted it back to us with a big out. I re-emphasize that the pitcher must keep in mind that he still must locate his fastball in a quality area on this pitch. To put it all in a nutshell, a pitcher can give the hitter what he's looking for, (fastball) but not on the timing he's synced to swing the bat. The timing the pitcher uses to offset the hitter's clicks or stride foot landing, causes his mind to send the signal to his hands to swing the bat a tad late. Since learning this technique and teaching it to my pitching staff, as well as Pat Borders using it in Major League games, we have witnessed a substantial amount of swings and misses on fastballs versus a solid contact or a game-changing swing of the bat that ultimately leads to losing a game.

When pitchers learn to apply this system, hitters have a tough time picking it up because we are doing it discretely and precisely picking and choosing when to use it, to which hitters to apply it to, and the hitters we need to make quality pitches to get out. Here is an example: How many times have we seen a hitter in such a groove, that no matter what pitch we make, he fouls 4, 5, 6, 7, 8 or even 9 to 10 pitches off. We as pitchers are so concerned in getting him out, we stay in his rhythm or clicks counts between pitches that we have allowed the hitter to stay in a groove. I challenge you to try and hold your count and watch the hitter get uncomfortable, offsetting his timing, and causing an out once we make the pitch. We can use this system creatively when a hitter shows he's in a groove. Apply it and see the amazing results you can achieve.

In the Major Leagues, certain pitchers use a different technique to keep hitters off balance. The pitchers I have seen use this unique timing technique are Johnny Cueto, Marcus Stroman, Kenley Jansen, Jeurys Familia. Johnny Cueto and Marcus Stroman use different speeds in their wind-up by adding a pause at the top of their leg lift or no pause at all. They keep hitters guessing to what delivery they are using, and it causes the hitter to be off timing putting their front foot down. The other speed they use is a quicker paced one. From the stretch, Jansen and Familia will come set hold the ball and pitch followed by no stopping at glove setting position and pitch (obviously with no runners on base). What they do and what I'm teaching in this chapter are both looking for the same result, to throw hitters timing off, and cause him to be late when the pitch is entering his solid contact zone.

I mentioned earlier in this chapter about the part of the brain called the **hypothalamus** and the human being in a state of **homeostasis**. I learned that a hitter's timing was disrupted if pitchers pitched the ball one second before the hitter's internal clock readjusted, which was at the 13-second mark. Then 12 seconds was the timing in which a pitcher should constantly work when sequencing pitches, pitch to pitch. In order to deliver the ball in 12 seconds or less, the pitcher must do a 3-step drop. The 3-step drop is when a pitcher lands with his follow-through foot, then walks backwards to the rubber. If it's a right-handed pitcher, once he's landed, it would be right, left, right, and should be back on the rubber receiving the ball from the catcher. This technique will have the pitcher deliver the baseball in 12 seconds or less. I was so intrigued by why this happened and the effect it had on hitters. I started to research and came across this vital information. The hypothalamus is the region of the forebrain below the thalamus that coordinates both the autonomic nervous system and the activity of the pituitary, controlling body temperature, thirst, hunger, and other homeostatic systems, and involved in sleep and emotional activity. The Central Nervous System (CNS) extends to the Peripheral Nervous System (PNF), a system of nerves that branch beyond the spinal cord, brain, and brainstem. The PNS carries information to and from the CNS. The Autonomic Nerves System (ANS) is further divided into the Sympathetic Nervous

System and the Parasympathetic Nervous System. The Sympathetic Nervous System is an involuntary system often associated with the flight or fight response, which is also associated with Adrenaline. The parasympathetic nervous system is responsible for promoting internal harmony such as a regular heartbeat during normal activity, which calms the hitter down. We are trying to prevent the hitter from refocusing and returning the hitter back in timing. Remember hitters need to step out of the box, adjust the batting glove, hit the bat against the inside cleats to dislodge dirt off the bottom of the spikes, and a certain bat pointing to pitcher once in the batter's box to be ready to hit. We as pitchers should understand how to disrupt these idiosyncrasies. As a student of the game, I researched the scientific point of view and learned how to understand it, teach it, and apply it with pitchers of all skill sets and levels with great success. We have heard that a baseball player doesn't need talent to hustle and this application goes with that phrase, a pitcher doesn't need to have talent to put this system into his arsenal as a competitor. Successful pitchers, who have achieved many levels of accomplishments, are always striving to get better. Baseball is a game of adjustments and a pitcher who has done something to better himself, adds a new dimension and or weapon to his game that the opposition must recognize, and then prepare. Adding a new dynamic to his pitching, the pitcher will be one step ahead of the competition, which is where the best competitors always want to be.

CHAPTER 12

Controlling the Running Game @ 1st Base and Right-handed Pitchers pickoff move

In 2013, I was the double AA pitching coach in Chattanooga, Tennessee and I was coupled with one of the coaches on staff during the Los Angeles Dodgers spring training of that year. My assignment and station were to control the running game at first base along with Davey Lopes. I worked with the pitchers and Davey worked with the runners as they rotated to our station. As I worked with all the left-handed pitchers in one of the stations, I was breaking down the pickoff move, and Davey was curious with something I was covering in the move. His questions opened a door for me to ask him questions I had on my mind about base runners. I asked him what made a good runner versus a bad runner and why holding the ball was so effective against potential base stealers? He proceeded to explain to me that the runners who have deficiencies are the ones that stand tall or are upright when taking leads. Those types of runners can get picked off due to bad mechanics. He mentioned that the ones that are usually good are the ones that are lower to the ground with feet apart and can change direction much easier than the ones with poor mechanics. He explained the way they should take leads with each step versus the one that is poor at it. Most runners are already in their max leads when the pitcher comes set versus the ones that stay on the bag longer and would jump off and get a late start and or lead off the pitcher. All this vital information allowed me to complete a system I had started to put together long before these great daily coaching sessions he and I had during spring training of that year. As pitchers, we want to develop the ability to control the running game, as it will help us give our team a chance to win especially close games as well as become a complete pitcher.

When controlling the running game at 1st base, a right-handed pitcher needs to work on improving two things, and that is quick feet and shorting or quickening up his arm range of motion. With the feet, the foot on the rubber steps off to the front of the rubber while the left foot gains ground towards 1st base. The lead foot gaining ground towards 1st base will prevent the pitcher from getting called for a balk.

To shorten his range of motion with his arm, the pitcher must keep the ball above the glove on hand separation and work on throwing with his hips, forearm, and hand to fingertips for a snap throw.

Once the pitcher gets his sign from the catcher, he looks at the runner at 1st and should not come set until the runner is in his full lead. The pitcher should not take his eyes off the runner as he's coming set, and if he takes a little more lead, the pitcher will know that he needs to pick to 1st when he sees this extra step. * **See figures 13-1 to 13-5**

If he's still on the bag and gets off late, then watch for him to cross his feet to attempt a quick pick move to 1st. When a runner takes his 2nd cross over step with the left foot just before it touches the ground, we can catch him off balance to get the right foot planted and make a move back to 1st.

We use the same approach with a runner that stays tall and brings feet together. We try and catch him just as his left foot is about to touch the ground to pick to 1st base. For a right-handed pitcher to control a good base stealer, he needs to do several things well.

1. The pitcher must be able to comfortably hold the ball or stay in his set position for 4 seconds or more. The reason is that a good base runner gets into his explosive get a good jump position with all his tension on his inner thighs down though inside of calves and to the instep of both feet. The longer the pitcher holds the ball, the more the runner holds that tension, it throws off his timing causing him to get a bad jump. An example is how runners in the Olympics get into the blocks waiting for the sound of the gun to go off, and someone jumps off and false starts. Holding the ball for 4 seconds disrupts the timing of the batter as well, as he wants the pitcher to load and go and pitch making it difficult for him to get ready to hit.

2. The pitcher should pick to 1st base with snap throw making runner fight to get back to the bag also with the 4-second hold.

3. The pitcher should have an excellent hold and step off making runner dive back to 1st because the pitcher was able to sell him a fake throw. You can accomplish this by turning from the waist up and right shoulder towards 1st base as you take your foot off behind the rubber with the ball up above your shoulder close to the right ear, and glove arm's elbow should be at the height of your shoulder also pointed towards 1st base. You are giving the illusion that you're going to throw to first but stopping on a dime causing the runner to dive hard and quick back to 1st base.

4. The pitcher should counter the 4-second hold with a 1-second hold and pitch as well as a 1-second hold and pick-off throw to 1st base. This will keep the runner off balance due to you holding the ball for 4 seconds before using this count.

5. The pitcher should always deliver the ball in 1.30 seconds or less to the plate. This time coupled with the catcher 's time of 2.00 and under should give him enough time to throw out runners trying to steal 2nd base. The reason we unload the ball in 1.30 and under to the plate is that the average runner gets to 2nd base in 3.3 seconds.

    a. This game is about advancement to the next base to create runs from an offensive point of view. We want to prevent runners at 1st from going 1st to 3rd with ease. We also will benefit on close plays at 2nd or making it difficult for a runner to break up double plays because we held him close enough to complete it and possibly get a pitcher, and the team out of a tough inning.

    b. Keep in mind good base stealers will try and steal on the first three pitches. The great base stealers will steal their bases, but when he faces you or your pitching staff, he will have a tough time getting a good jump and deal with you unloading the ball quickly to the plate effecting his success. If we disrupt his timing, we have a chance to get him thrown out at 2nd or 3rd base.

6. Ferguson Jenkins once said when runners reach 1st they have a 25% chance on scoring. When they get to 2nd it goes up to 50%, and when they get to 3rd base, it goes up to 75% that they can score.

7. Developing this approach will give you the best chances to be a *WINNING PITCHER!*

RHP PICK OFF MOVE TO FIRST BASE

WHEN COMING SET PITCHER KEEPS THE RUNNER IN HIS PERIPHERAL VISION. CHIN IS ON FRONT SHOULDER & PUPIL ON THE CORNER OF YOUR EYE

BACK FOOT REPLACES FRONT FOOT AS THE FRONT FOOT GAINS GROUND TOWARDS FIRST BASE TO PREVENT FROM BEING CALLED FOR A BALK

Figure 13-1

RHP PICK OFF MOVE TO FIRST BASE

EYES LOCK IN ON TARGET QUICKLY TO MAKE AN ACCURATE THROW

PITCHER ALSO NEEDS TO HAVE QUICK FEET ACTION REPLACING FRONT FOOT WITH BACK FOOT AS WE CONTINUE TO GAIN GROUND TOWARDS FIRST BASE

PITCHER SHOULD KEEP HIS HANDS ABOVE THE SHOULDER SHORTING UP HIS RANGE OF MOTION. WE NEED TO HAVE SHORT, & QUICK MOVEMENTS WITH GLOVE & THROWING HAND

Figure 13-2

Figure 13-3

Figure 13-4

Figure 13-5

CHAPTER 13

Left-Handed Pick Off Move

As a former left-handed pitcher, I was not blessed with a natural pickoff move. Like everything else in pitching, it was a part of my game I needed to develop. My pickoff move was developed through curiosity and a desire to pick runners off.

In the summer of 1987 Everyday early in the season during batting practice I would go to centerfield and ask my teammate and former big leaguer Milt Cuyler if he could watch my pickoff move and see what he could pick up to help me get better at it. He would simulate the base runner at first, and I would go through my pickoff move then would phantom a pitch to the plate. I did this with him for about two weeks straight. We did this routine daily, and he was ironing out whatever flaw I had in my pickoff move. By the end of those two weeks, he couldn't make out if I was going home with a pitch or coming over to first base with my best move. I decided it was now time to try it in a game to the first batter that reached first base. My career changed from that moment in that game, as I picked off the first batter to reach first base.

Another one of my teammates and former big leaguer Ron Rightnowar who saw me pick off the runner excitedly came to me and explained how I needed a routine to hide my best move. Once he explained what he meant, I worked on it diligently and I went on to pick off 18 runners at first base during the South Atlantic League campaign in 1987. I always wondered if I hadn't developed that pickoff move how differently that season and my career would've been and how much higher my ERA of 2.79 might have ended up.

The work and attention to detail that went into developing this part of my game were paramount. I did not have the slightest idea how much it would be an important facet for a winning pitcher. Controlling base runners by varying my times and being quick to the plate was just a part of it. Developing a good pickoff move was the icing on the cake. I felt that I could intimidate runners because I was so efficient in my system, which, I will share in detail.

As we embark on this part of the game with left-handed pitchers, know that we have a tremendous advantage seeing the runners right in front of you. We can pick up runners' tendencies and how they can tip off what they are about to do, so we can be equipped to counter it to get them thrown out at 2nd base. As I became better in this area, it made the rest of the game easier.

When a left-handed pitcher works on his pickoff move, the first thing we should have in mind is making our best move to first as identical to or as close to our delivery to the plate as possible.

There is no such thing as a 45-degree angle in the rulebook, but there is a fine line as to where you can land with your right foot to avoid being called for a balk by the umpire. You can draw the 45-degree angle for working purposes and get the pitcher comfortable with his direction to first. What umpires look at from a left-handed pitcher attempting a pickoff to first base is space between his left foot on the rubber and right foot landing towards first base. The other action they look for is if the left-handed pitcher crosses his right leg past the left leg to attempt a pickoff to first base and it's seen from the umpire on the bases. *See figure 14-1

As we've covered in the pitching from the stretch section of this book, pitchers start by leading with their hips, meaning the lower half. By the lower half starting first, the head naturally stays over the back foot causing hand separation to happen simultaneously. As this happens, it gives the left-handed pitcher complete control of his body, which he can take in any direction home or to first base. The back foot controls his direction as it is recommended to keep your heel on the ground so you can to create that angle towards where you want to go. *See figure 14-2

One of the common flaws left-handed pitchers have when making a move towards first base is, since the lower half doesn't control their direction, they over rotate with their front shoulder causing the back shoulder to go back in the direction of third base and they telegraph the pickoff move immediately. It's a completely different motion than one used to deliver a pitch. The pitcher that has this type of flaw doesn't lead with his lower half to the plate.

To avoid the shoulders from over rotating towards first base, the pitcher must do the first part of the delivery correctly, and it will keep his head over the back foot. By staying over the back foot, the shoulders will stay in line with home plate causing the runner to hold his position because you've broken the plane where runners think you're going home with the pitch. *See figure 14-3

This will also give the pitcher time to get his arm into throwing position without giving away where he's throwing the ball to, which ultimately should look like he's making a pitch to the plate.

When hand separation occurs, the glove hand should go to the same place a pitcher has it in when one is making a pitch to the plate. This will also help in the pitchers' alignment between ball and glove in direction with 2nd base and home plate when a runner is looking at you.

As the pitcher gets his hand out of the glove, he should visualize throwing the ball when he's about to release it. The head is facing home when making a pitch and it should be the same facing home until the last possible second. *See figure 14-4

This will help him take the ball out of the glove and start a complete circle of down, up, and release point. Most left-handed pitchers think about throwing the ball too early leading to tipping off his pickoff move by turning his shoulders. The only time a pitcher looks to first should be as he's releasing the ball. *See figure 14-5

Another piece of the pickoff move that is important is release and follow through. If the pitcher does the leading with lower half or hips and has hand separation, then drive towards first base with backside and making sure the heal stays down, then he needs to think like he's making a pitch to first base. What that means is that your finish should simulate the finish you have when making a pitch to the plate. If you ride out the backside down the slope towards first base, it will feel as if you are making a pitch to the first baseman without the velocity. It will also enable one to make the pick-off attempt late as appose to early, maintaining the deception. * See figure 14-6

A good way to maintain deception with a good move is with head movement. I recommend that if the pitcher is going to first base with anything other than his best move, the pitcher should look to first as he makes his pick-off attempt. (Come set looking at the runner and throw without looking towards home plate).

On the other hand, if the pitcher is using his best move, then he should be looking home until the last possible second before his pick-off attempt. Looking home as soon as you go into your knee or leg lift is the precise time you should pick up the plate and keep that head angle until the release of the pick-off attempt. The routine to set up your best move goes as follows:

The first thing we want to show is that the left-handed pitcher shows a well below average move to first base. Usually, you will get the coach from third base scream across the infield to the runner at first that the pitcher has a better move than the one he just used, so heads up. They do not want a runner to get careless and get picked off. With this below average type of move, we recommend that the pitcher use his right shoulder and right foot and align it towards first base when making his pick-off attempt. The runner will see your front side coming towards him. This is completely different from the pitchers best move because we're using the backside, which helps to hide a pitcher's best move.

With the runner at first still looking for your best move, the pitcher has an opening to attack the hitter to get ahead of the count. The hitters usually give a base stealer two or three pitches to steal the bag. They try and allow a base runner to be on second so; he can drive him in for an RBI. It is vital that we throw a strike to stay in control of the situation as we put pressure on the hitter as well. We can use a high leg lift and we're counting that the runner is still looking for your best move.

Next, we recommend the pitcher do a slide step directly towards first base as he's doing his pick-off attempt. By doing a slide step towards first base mentally, the runner begins to think the pitcher doesn't have a good pickoff move. What are the thoughts that might go through his mind? He goes over the sequence the pitcher used and makes mental notes. More importantly the one time the pitcher went to home plate with a pitch he had a higher leg lift and looked home. When the pitcher came to first, he was looking in the direction of the runner. (A slide step is not having much of a leg lift to be quick to the plate). In this case, we're slide-stepping to first base. The runner starts to gain confidence thinking he has your move, which in this case isn't good for the runner, but SURPRISE you give him your best pickoff move.

Based on these sequences of moves to first base and pitch to the plate it has prepared you as a left-handed pitcher to reveal or unveil your best move.

Now with your best move remember we will show the runner the delivery we used to make a pitch to the plate. When going to the plate, we picked up home plate immediately as we started our leg lift. We start to lead with our hips or lower half combined with hand separation the runner at this point sees us going home with the pitch. It imperative that we ride out that backside as long as we can down the slope towards first base causing a late read and runner gets a bad jump on his way to second base. We as pitchers do not pick up the first baseman until we are about to throw him the ball. The magic word is SURPRISE! A caught stealing! Runner gets tagged out at second base by the shortstop.

Using this same technique, we must incorporate a pickoff move from the slide step move. This sequence is to be mixed around once an opposing team has seen us use it against them. One of the great things that we will learn from developing a good pickoff move is the action's runners do and how they tip off when they are about to take off and try to steal a base. Being efficient with this system will allow a pitcher to be able to counter any move a runner makes.

It is very important the left-handed pitchers do not break the plane of his back leg with his right foot, or the pitcher will get called for a balk advancing the runner into scoring position. The right foot can come just inside in front of the left knee or leg, but if it goes past it, then a balk call is in order.

If we as pitchers know that a runner at first likes to peak in to steal the signs from the catcher, here is a technique one can use to let him know he's peeking. We usually get our sign from the catcher with maybe our glove on right knee and ball behind your left hamstring muscle. We then come to our set position looking at the runner at first base. To counter runners peeking, have in mind that his helmet is facing you the pitcher, but his eyes are peeking to the catcher's signs as the pitcher is also getting his signs from that same catcher. The runner is waiting for your big movement to make you think he's locked in on you and before you come to your set position look from getting the sign from the catcher to looking at him directly, I can a sure you that you will catch the runner at first base peeking in for the signs.

How can peeking in for signs work against a pitcher? Let's say we have a 1-2 count, and the pitcher is throwing a curveball down in the dirt for a put away he can anticipate the curveball bouncing in the dirt and take off stealing second base. Another reason the runners will straight steal is with the knowledge that an off-speed pitch was being made. The last action I will cover about the pickoff move is the hold and step off move. What I learned about runners at first is that they sometimes have a one-way lead back to the bag enticing you to pick to analyze a deficiency in your movements. When a pitcher picks this up from the mound, he should step off hard and quick, twisting with the front, or right shoulder and elbow raised as if you were going to make a throw, but stopped on a dime causing the runner at first to dive back with a tremendous amount of urgency and effort. Even though you never threw the ball, you sold it as you were throwing and did not. You have won a small mental battle due to making him dive back suckering him into doing something, but something else happened. He must now get up, dust himself off and dislodge any dirt that's inside of pants waist without a throw ever being made. It can set up a step off snap throw as he might be caught sleeping or lack of aggression diving back the second time.

We can't emphasize enough how vital a pickoff move is to your success. The ultimate objective is to keep runners close and from getting good jumps to second. It will pay dividends when your middle infielders turn a double play without it being broken up. You can make a tough play in the hole and still get a runner thrown out at second base.

Giving catchers enough time to throw base runners out. Great pitchers understand the importance of controlling base runners. It is one of the major reasons they are winners!

Figure 14-1

Figure 14-2

Figure 14-3

Figure 14-4

Figure 14-5

Figure 14-6

CHAPTER 14

Controlling the Running Game @ 2nd Base-With the halfway look

When a pitcher has a runner on 2nd, there are tendencies runners have that indicate what he is about to do. What are those tendencies?

A pitcher should always identify what type of runner is on the base. (Burner, base stealer, or a truck).

He should remember runners are taught not to make the 1st or the 3rd out at 3rd base. The *pitcher should not be neglectful based on this unwritten rule.*

Keep in mind runners steal from 2nd when they see the back of your head. By being in the halfway look, the runner can't see the back of your head, and they know you have them in your view. Lastly, it's easier to pick up home plate from that head position.

When making a pitch to the plate, a pitcher should still deliver the ball in 1.30 seconds, and that is one of the biggest reasons' runners would be very hesitant to run. Average runners are 3.3 seconds on steal attempts.

When a pitcher is coming set, he should be looking to second and pick up the runner visually. Once he picks up the runner, he looks in the direction of 3rd base. This is what's called the *halfway look.* When in this position pitcher should be looking back to 2nd from the corner of his eye to enhance his peripheral vision.

If the runner is just relaxed without a big lead, he should throw a strike from the *halfway look* head position.

When coming set and picking up the runner, if the runner is jockeying back and forth the base *runner is mostly just trying to throw off the pitcher's rhythm and focus on the hitter.* The pitcher should let this runner jockey all he wants from the halfway look when he gets too far from the base; he will take a step or two back towards 2nd and pitcher delivers a strike. *Runners can't steal a base going back to second.* You should do a great job of focusing on making a quality pitch when you've committed to going home.

When coming set and picking up the runner go into the halfway look, the runner is taking calculated shuffle steps *red flag* should indicate runner is thinking of timing you and attempt a steal. When you see this the *Daylight play with the shortstop or 2nd baseman is in place.* You will be in perfect synchronization with the infielder and possibly pick the runner off. Both you and the infielder will know that's the time to do the daylight pickoff play and beating the runner back to the bag.

Just like pitchers tipping off pitches, runners also tip off when they are going to steal. Runners sometimes do different things when they are about to steal. We as pitchers need to pay close attention to detail. A tip a runner will send you will be the wiggling his fingers, and before that, they were not wiggling.

Another tip is getting lower and in a more explosive position to get a good jump. Getting anxious and flinching to run before you deliver the ball is another tip. The pitcher in a halfway look picking this up knows the *inside move* will be in place so the runner can take off *and fall into an easy trap* of getting caught between the base path. The *inside move* should be deliberate and *easy to sell to the runner* that you are making a pitch allowing him to get a good jump, but *Surprise!*

With the inside move, the pitcher should come up to a balanced position on knee lift and start his rotational move to 2nd on the way down. He should avoid taking his front side towards 2nd base because runner will be tipped off and shut down the steal attempt, which should give you an out without making a pitch. The key is to sell that you are going home, so going up and down in a balanced position should make you a great salesman. Anytime we get an out, without making a pitch is a big bonus and they are very hard to come by.

Once you've established the halfway look and then do a no-look, a pitcher can then look to 2nd base pick up the runner and look home to make the pitch. The beautiful thing about this system is that the runner is expecting you to look towards 3rd in a halfway look position and it never happened. It's like the train left the station and he wasn't on it only because you've done a good job establishing the halfway look. The pitcher will be making pitches without any worries of the runner stealing because he will be so off timing that he's stuck in quicksand.

The *No-Look* is the last part of this system that throws off runners' timing at 2nd. With the no-look pitcher comes set, this time looking home. We pause to let the runner know we are in the no-look position as he probably recognizes it and might want to take off, but then you turn your head and pick him up, and it freezes him. Next, go into the halfway look seeing runner from the corner of your eye and when comfortable throw a strike.

You can now do the *no look* without *pausing much* and throw a strike. It is important to pause briefly because the last time you did the no look, you had a longer pause. By the time he recognizes that you were in the no look, you were already throwing a strike to the plate. The key is a brief pause.

This system is designed merely for pitchers to have complete control of runners at 2nd base. It enhances your ability to be a winning pitcher, especially in close games.

Paying attention to detail is the hallmark of a winning pitcher.

With practice of this system, you will become an expert on how to control runners and be the pitcher everyone wants on their team.

CHAPTER 15

Methods to Prevent stealing signs from 2nd Base

We as pitchers need to always protect ourselves from coaches who steal our catcher's signs to relay them back to the hitter from one of the coaches' boxes. Another way signs are relayed with a runner on 1st is peeking from the corner of his eyes while looking at the pitcher to see catcher's signs, so they can anticipate an off-speed pitch is being thrown hopefully in the dirt so they can steal 2nd base.

This segment will cover runners at 2nd base relaying signs or location back to the hitter so they can hit your best-executed pitches. It is a part of the game that isn't talked about much, but when it happens, and pitchers do not counter their relaying of signs, lots of solid contacts, and big hits occur during a game once runners reach 2nd base.

What do we mean regarding runners stealing signs? When a runner reaches 2nd base, they are taught to pay attention and read the catchers' signs back to the pitcher. They see if, for example, your catcher puts down one finger for a fastball as the first pitch and if the pitcher throws it, they know it is the first sign. (Keep in mind we're talking about a set of 3 to 4 sign sequence). If the same thing happens with the 2nd or the 3rd sign and the pitcher throws that pitch the runner at 2nd base has your signs.

Another thing to look for is the runner at 2nd base relaying to the hitter the location of the pitch that is about to be thrown. The runner at 2nd base does certain gestures back to the hitter that will indicate on what side of the plate the pitch will be thrown. If a pitcher is pitching a good game, but something different happens as far as a hitter's driving in runners easily from 2nd base, then we need to have in mind that the other team might be stealing signs. If this is happening, then what are the signs that are being relayed to give hitters the information that distinguishes what pitch or location is coming?

Let's first touch on runners relaying location. There are several body gestures that runner tips off to the hitter that a pitch is in a certain location.

One of the methods used by runners to relay signs to the hitter is by looking towards 2nd base, which will indicate to the hitter that the pitch is away to a right-handed hitter. Once the pitcher comes set looking at the runner, the runner looks in the direction of 2nd base, and if the pitcher is throwing a pitch away, then a red flag should be raised that they are possibly giving away your location. If he looks towards 3rd base then, the pitch location will be to the inside part of the plate to that same right-handed hitter.

A method they also use is by sticking a finger in either side of the helmet ear hole to indicate inside or outside of the strike zone.

Another method used by runners to relay signs to the hitter is when the runner at 2nd base has his feet set and his hands on his knees. Once the pitcher comes set and looks towards him at 2nd, he starts his first movement with his left foot to get into his maximum lead; then if a right-handed hitter is up at the plate, the location is away. On the other hand, if he starts his first movement with his right foot (the one closest to 3rd), then the location will be inside.

They can also have one hand hanging down and the other on the hip or knee to indicate inside or outside location. When the runner's left hand is hanging down, the location is away to a right-handed hitter, and if the right hand is hanging down, then the location is inside to the right-handed hitter.

A couple of different methods used by runners to relay a certain pitch to the hitter is when having his hands on his knees in a fist indicating a fastball is coming. If the runner has his hands off his knees hanging down and wiggling his fingers, this will indicate an off-pitch will be thrown.

When facing a team that is very good at stealing signs, they will do a combination of things to relay location as well as the pitch. We must do our due diligence to be one step ahead of the competition to not fall into the trap of being prey to these intelligent players who will do anything to get an edge to win a game.

The suggestions we use below are to give you sequences that work and will keep the pitcher in tune with these intricacies of the game at the higher levels of baseball. This is not to say that they are not using these methods at the college levels or below. We as competitors should have in mind that most athletes are always trying to get an edge and this awareness will prevent any opposing team from taking advantage of your natural gifts and talents. As we have mentioned before if you get beat, it should be because you were outpitched not because you were not prepared.

SEQUENCES TO USE WITH A MAN ON 2ND BASE:

With Men on 2nd base:

Use four signs

If pitcher shakes, use last sign and only give three signs

Sequences:

1st sign—1st sign of sequence is live

2nd sign—2nd sign of sequence is live

Last sign—last sign of sequence is live

ABE (Ahead, Even, Behind):

On all counts we are ahead of hitter (0-1,0-2,1-2) 1st sign is live.

On all counts we are Even (0-0,1-1,2-2) 3rd sign is live.

On all counts we are Behind (1-0,2-0,3-0,2-1,3-1,3-2) 2nd sign is live.

The Outs + 1 Sequence:

0 outs-1st sign, 1 out-2nd sign, 2 outs-3rd sign.

Hot and Live Signs

1st sign after 2 or after 3—The sign immediately follows either a 2 or 3 depending on which is the hot sign.

1st sign indicator—1st sign tells you how many signs to count after to determine which is the live sign.

For example:

The sequence is: "2-1-3-4" 2 is the indicator, and the live sign is 3.

If the sequence is: "3-4-1-2" 3 is the indicator, and the live sign is 2.

If the sequence is: "1-4-2-1" 1 is the indicator, and the live sign is 4.

1st sign after last pitch—The last pitch thrown when man got to 2nd base is then used as the hot sign, and the sign following that sign is the pitch. For example, Batter hits a slider for a double (3) the hot sign for the next batter would be 3. So, if the sequence is 2-1-3-1 it would be 1. Next pitch, 1-4-2-3 would be 4. Then, 1-4-3-2 would be 3, etc.

Pumps—The number of pumps is what the pitch is. 1 pump FB, 2 pumps CB, 3 pumps SL, etc. Note the actual signs do not mean anything only the number of pumps you see.

# of touches to equipment—Using left shin guard, mask, chest and right shin guard as hot spots, the number of times you touch the equipment is the pitch like the pump's method. The actual fingers you put down do not mean anything.

# of touches to equipment indicator—The number of touches to the hot spots mentioned above is the indicator for the actual signs. For example, if you touch mask, and chest, then it would be 2nd sign. If you touched just mask, it would be 1st sign, etc. The signs vary from pitch to pitch.

Area of equipment—Each hot spot is a pitch. For example, left shin guard for FB, mask for CB, chest for the slider, and right shin guard for a changeup. The fingers you put down don't mean anything. You can use 1st or last touch as the active spot so you can give multiple signs. If using the last touch in the sequence mask, chest, mask, right shin guard, the pitch would be change up.[4]

The most difficult one is the roller over system.

In this system, the pitches go as follows.

Curveball 1- Fastball away 2 - Slider 3 - Change-up 4 -Fastball inside 5

The signs go up to the 5th sign then rolls over back to the first sign. Remembering each number and what pitch it is will keep this system simple.

The indicator is the first sign the catcher puts down. After the indicator is given, then we start to count pumps. If he puts down one finger, the pitcher then counts how many pumps after that indicator.

For example, the catcher puts down two fingers which is the indicator, then gives you three pumps, then the pitch is a fastball inside.

If the catcher puts down three fingers, three is the indicator followed by three pumps then the pitch would be a curveball. Remember once the indicator, which was three, followed by three pumps we ended based on the rollover back to the first sign, which was one, the curveball.

One more example, the catcher puts down four fingers followed by three pumps. Four was the indicator, and three pumps meant 4-5 rollover-1-2 fastball away is the pitch.

To keep this system running smoothly between the pitcher and catcher the pitcher can wipe with his glove up by the chest to add a number or wipe down by his thigh to subtract a pitch from the catcher's final pump.

For example, the catcher puts down one finger followed by two pumps which is a slider, but the pitcher wants to throw a fastball away, he then wipes one time on his thigh meaning subtract one which will now make the pitch a fastball away. If the catcher puts down one finger followed by two pumps, he wants a slider, but the pitcher wants to throw a change-up, then the pitchers wipe on his chest one time to go up one, and that will now make the pitch a change-up.

Before implementing this system, the coach will have to take all pitchers and catchers to practice this meticulously until achieving perfection. We want to avoid catchers being crossed up and prevent any type of injuries due to miscommunication.

These are just possible suggestions and if you have something else just make sure the pitcher and catcher can do it as a unit.

CHAPTER 16

Peak Performance Triangle / TRIANGLE OF SUCCESS

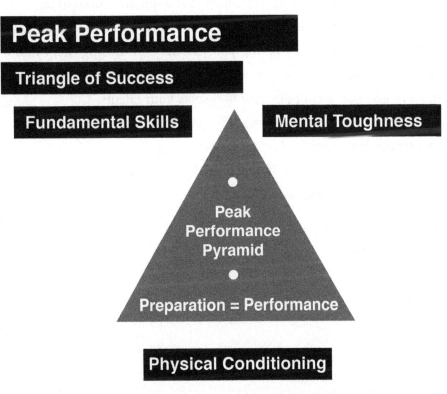

Peak Performance

Triangle of Success

Fundamental Skills

Mental Toughness

Peak Performance Pyramid

Preparation = Performance

Physical Conditioning

Bridge the gap between potential and performance
"TALENT VS PERFORMANCE"

The peak performance triangle is a way to show pitchers the whole pie broken down into all its pieces. Pitchers get a good grasp of what it all entails to be a complete pitcher. Here we have a breakdown of all the pitchers' responsibilities and looking at it from this perspective; it puts it in a simplistic way, so the pitcher can see how many areas he needs to excel at being successful. When pitchers look at the peak performance triangle, we want to avoid them taking any one area for granted which goes with the saying, "get beat because you were outpitched, not because you weren't prepared."[5]

The three areas are fundamental skills, mental toughness, and physical conditioning. We learn that talent isn't enough to get you by; it's the preparation combined with the talent that leads to positive results in your performances. Potential is also not enough. The meaning of potential is having or showing the capacity to become or develop into something in the future. It sounds like hope for the future. We as pitchers need to have the presence in mind to take that potential and develop it into a solid career based on your performances through your preparation, by taking your talents and turning them into a skill. Then sandlot teams, high schools, colleges, and possibly the professional level will take you serious enough to give you an opportunity to display your talents.

For the professional pitcher, The Peak Performance Triangle is a way of life. The more successful pitcher you are, the more you live by this system.

We need to be fully engaged in each specific area, and it will breed in you a fearless competitor with a winning attitude that is second to none.

CHAPTER 17

Fundamental Skills

Fundamental Skills

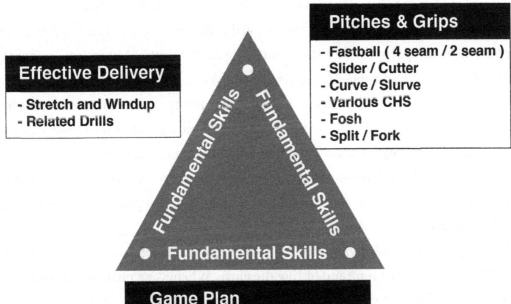

Pitches & Grips

- Fastball (4 seam / 2 seam)
- Slider / Cutter
- Curve / Slurve
- Various CHS
- Fosh
- Split / Fork

Effective Delivery

- Stretch and Windup
- Related Drills

Game Plan

- Long Toss Throwing Program
- Warm-up Routine
- Starter / Reliever
- Control Running Game
- Excecute the Gameplan

[5]The fundamental skill is the area in which we can always improve on having a better delivery or maintaining a good one. Having a good routine that includes going through your delivery without a ball and substituting it with a towel for resistance to do enough repetitions that will become second nature when you pitch. Hitters can swing the bat all day during their workouts, pitchers, on the other hand, can only throw a baseball a limited amount of times before he enters the danger zone of possible injuries. Drills allow a pitcher to work on strengthening his deficiencies with a substantial amount of repetitions with or without a towel in his hand.

Working on your different grips is vital to your development. When playing catch with your throwing partner, we can experiment with a fastball on using both types of grips. For young pitchers, we recommend using a four-seam grip, but as we mature a two-seam grip will be important when needing a ground ball for a possible double play to get you out of a jam or simply induce a ball on the ground with the infield in or in a shift, etc.

The slider or cutter is important pitches we need to throw for strikes and learn to expand the strike zone making it look like a strike but being a ball to entice hitters into swinging at it for a put-away. This also applies to curveballs and slurves.

The Change-ups is the pitch with the lowest batting average against because hitters have a difficult time recognizing it. The change-up is a pitch most pitchers try to master last in their repertoire and if they knew early on, how many easy outs and swings and misses they would get with the change-up, one would think they would've worked on it much earlier in their career or development. The change-up comes in different grips like the Split finger, Forkball, Fosh, and Circle Change.

Having a game plan and having the ability to execute your pitches is vital. It all comes from making one pitch at a time and hitting the glove. Whenever a pitcher is in the stretch, he should always be working on delivering the pitch on 1.30 seconds to the plate and making it a quality pitch. We do not want the game to speed up on you due to only being 1.30 during games, but not in your practice bullpen routines.

Warm-up routine is a pitcher's lifeline. All great athletes have great routines. Routines help you stay focused with minimal to no distractions. Routines allow you to focus on the task at hand and execute.

Controlling the running game at both 1st and 2nd base falls squarely on the pitcher's shoulder. Fergurson Jenkins once said that once a runner reaches 1st base, he has a 25% chance of scoring. Once he reaches 2nd base, he has a 50% chance of scoring and once he reaches 3rd base that number goes up to a 75% chance. The game of baseball is repetition, and I will repeat myself quite often throughout this system because so many things in the game intertwine.

Perfect practice makes perfect, and if you take our warm-up routines with this mentality, they will improve daily. We can't emphasize enough how important it is to command your pitches during your flat ground and warm-up pitch routines. We are always striving for perfection and rarely attain it for long periods of time in baseball, but a conditioned mind, always working towards it, will pay tremendous dividends.

Remember a starter and a reliever are different animals. Know what it takes, to do your job to get the most out of your ability, to help your team win games. Winning is a by-product of fundamentals and preparation.

Long Toss throwing programs should always be designed to simulate your delivery. All your throwing programs should be geared to enhance and re-enforce your pitches off the mound. A long-toss program shouldn't be to see how far you could throw a baseball; it should be to make you a better pitcher and keep in mind that good pitchers throw quality strikes consistently.

Another important aspect of pitching is doing your delivery in front of a mirror or off the mound with a towel or without. It's essential for us pitchers to know ourselves and to understand our mechanics from the inside out so we can concentrate on just making pitches and getting hitters out in games.

CHAPTER 18

Mental Toughness

Mental Toughness

- Concentration

- Active Visualization

- Relaxation

- Composure

- Pressure Situations

- Stay Cool, Calm, and Collected

- Video Training

- Pre-Pitch Routines

- Motivation

- Goal Setting

- Smart Goals

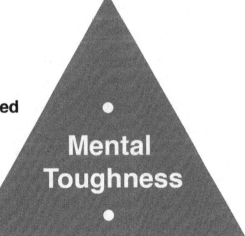

Concentration is vital to a pitcher's success. Deep concentration in all areas is paramount. Being a perfectionist through your ability to focus and concentrate will get a pitcher to where he wants to be, and that is being consistent.

Active visualization: A study was done of players doing their regular practice routine and then playing the games. Another group of players did the same but added active visualization to their routine, and they performed better in games than the ones that didn't do it. Active visualization is a powerful tool we must take advantage of to be excellent at our craft. Visualization and mental imagery are forms of experience. Visualize the mound, the grass, home plate, catchers' shoes, shin guards, laces inside his glove, light coming through his webbing, the baseball and its seams, the Rawlings logo, making a well-located pitch, throwing your curveball or slider for strikes, expanding the strike zone in the dirt, and a fastball above the bat with two strikes for a strikeout. Visualize getting easy outs or ugly swings and misses with a change-up. Visualize the batters you will be facing and pitch for pitch how you will get them out. See yourself releasing the ball where you want to throw a quality strike, a double play situation, and making the pitch to get a ball on the ground resulting in two outs with one pitch. With two strikes on the hitter, see yourself making that perfect pitch to strike him out--these visuals one can see and gain subconscious confidence without even making a pitch.

Being relaxed under pressure is a quality we must learn to develop, and it all starts with breathing. If we are hyperventilating, it's impossible to be relaxed. Breathing under control will keep your muscles relaxed and mind clear in the most pressure situations that we encounter in games.

Composure is the ability to stay the same no matter what the score or the situation of the game is. Never let them see you sweat is the key. Keeping your emotions in check is a fine art a pitcher can acquire in bullpen sessions. It can also be practiced before games during the flat ground throwing program. Simulate game-like situations, and if executed in practice, it will transition into your games.

Making pitches in pressure situations is an art that's practiced constantly during all your routines--bullpens sessions, flat ground throwing program, visualization and then finally doing it in games. Always hitting the glove is the basic principle without the hitter being a factor. Staying cool, calm, and collected all the time is a practiced art.

Video sessions are a way of life in the game of baseball today. Studying other line-ups and dissecting opposing hitters' swings and strength and weaknesses is part of a pitcher's preparation.

Pre-pitch routines are what keeps a pitcher on having good rhythm and

tempo and keeps a game flowing at a nice pace. Remember we want to make hitters uncomfortable by working quickly between pitches. It will also help you focus and concentrate from pitch to pitch with ease.

Motivation comes in different forms, but the most important one is self-motivation. The desire comes from deep down inside your gut. A pitcher needs to have three things in order, his mind, his heart, and his guts to be complete.

Goal setting is important because it will get you to where you want to go. A ship at sea without a destination is just a ship at sea.

Smart goals should be in place for a pitcher to go about his business in a systematic way to get the most out of your ability.

CHAPTER 19

Physical Conditioning

Physical Conditioning

- Endurance

- Power

- Strength

- Plyometric

Medicine Ball - Throws / Twists

- Weight Training

- Rotator Cuff

- Elbow Program

- Aerobic/ Anaerobic Training Program

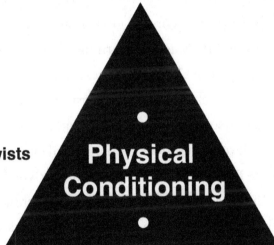

Endurance training is the act of exercising to increase endurance. The term endurance training generally refers to training the aerobic system as opposed to anaerobic. The need for endurance in sports is often predicated as the need for cardiovascular and simple muscular endurance, but the issue of endurance is far more complex. Endurance can be divided into two categories including general endurance and specific endurance. It can be shown that endurance in sports is closely tied to the execution of skill and technique. A well-conditioned athlete can be defined as the athlete who executes his or her technique consistently and effectively with the least effort.

Power: the ability to exert maximum muscular contraction instantly in an explosive burst of movements. The two components of power are strength and speed. (e.g., jumping or a sprint)

Strength: the extent to which muscles can exert force by contracting against resistance (e.g., holding or restraining an object or person)

Plyometrics, also known as "jump training" or "plyos", are exercises based around having muscles exert maximum force in short intervals of time to increase both speed and power. This training focuses on learning to move from a muscle extension to a contraction in a rapid or "explosive" manner, for example with specialized repeated jumping.

We as pitchers rely on interval explosiveness from pitch to pitch. Plyometrics works on building that explosiveness by working our lower half as well as core and arm strengthening exercises to develop our total abilities and talents.

Medicine Ball; We should keep in mind the "core" is comprised of more than just the abs muscles. The core includes the lower back, upper back, groin, and hips. Any baseball core routine should be designed to strengthen these muscles. We as pitchers have a tremendous amount of rotational movements as we throw the baseball and the medicine ball exercises will strengthen this so important muscle group.

Rotator Cuff. The rotator cuff consists of four muscles that act together to stabilize and move the shoulder joint. Due to the function of these muscles, in a sport, which require demanding overhead activities, such as baseball, put the rotator cuff muscles under an undue amount of stress especially if mechanically the pitcher is out of sync.[6]

Elbow Maintenance Program is vital for keeping the elbow and surrounding muscles strong. With the combination of a good elbow weight program and proper mechanics, the pitcher should be able to stay healthy during the season.

Anaerobic /Aerobic Training Program

Anaerobic training increases the athlete's anaerobic capacity by increasing their lactate tolerance, the size of the fast-twitch muscle fibers, and the resting levels of ATP, Creatine Phosphate, free Creatine, and glycogen in the athlete's muscles.

The aerobic system is used to power steady-state exercise of continuous duration of longer than 3-to-4 minutes. Aerobic capacity is increased through interval training, continuous training (this must be intense enough to overload the aerobic system), and fartlek training. Aerobic training increases aerobic capacity through adaptations to the athlete's oxygen transport and utilization systems.

Both the anaerobic and aerobic power systems are important to the athlete ad each needs to be trained to optimize their athletic performance.[7]

CHAPTER 20

Smart Goals

Process vs outcome

"Without goals and plans to reach them, you are like a ship at sea that has set sail with no destination."

SMART GOALS

Specific	Have a greater chance of being accomplished than general goals
Measurable	How much? How many times? How will I know when it's accomplished?
Attainable	Attitudes, Abilities, Skills
Realistic	Need to be willing and able, goals can be high
Timely	Need time frame for sense of urgency! Loose 10lbs when? Some day will not work...By April 1st

Once a pitcher has grasped the system, then how will he manage himself within it? Smart goals are a way for him to mentally organize his vision of how he will attain his goals.

The first thing we want to convey is how to use the smart goals correctly. This is a way to hold the pitcher accountable to his progress and development and to show him how to achieve his goals in a smart way.[8]

CHAPTER 21

Four Elements of Pitching

1. LOCATION:

   a. Location is number one because a pitcher can win at any level by locating two or more pitches in the strike zone as well as having the ability to expand the limits of the strike zone

2. CHANGE OF SPEEDS:

   a. Changing speed is the second way a pitcher can dominate the hitter is by adding and subtracting velocity with location. Hitting is timing and changing speeds throws off timing.

3. MOVEMENT:

   a. Movement with location, gets hitters out by making a hitter not center the ball, therefore making poor contact.

4. VELOCITY:

   a. Velocity with poor location is a recipe for failure.

   b. Location and Changing speeds with late Movement are the key elements for success at the Major League level.

5. THE VARIABLES OF PITCHING

a. In and Out / Up and Down / Back and Forth

b. When elite pitchers at ML level get their checks, they say HMM! Location lots of $$$

CHAPTER 22

Controlling the Count

Controlling the Count

Pitchers	Record	H/9	SO/9	BB/9	Earnings
Lincecum, Tim	80-46	7.6	9.1	3.5	$81,055,000
Cain, Matt	85-80	7.5	7.5	3.1	$71,744,666
Suppan, Jeff	140-146	10.1	4.9	3.1	$58,125,000
Lilly, Ted	130-111	8.3	7.6	3.0	$80,439,816
Myers, Bret	97-95	9.1	7.3	2.9	$59,257,499
Pettitte, Andy	247-142	9.3	6.7	2.8	$139,832,416
Harang, Aaron	105-105	9.4	7.3	2.7	$54,150,000
Beckett, Josh	132-97	8.3	8.3	2.7	$116,465,264
Lackey, John	128-95	9.4	7.1	2.7	$108,036,666
Santana, Johan	139-78	9.7	8.8	2.5	$161,497,269
Carpenter, Chris	144-94	8.9	6.9	2.5	$98,592,956
Weaver, Jared	102-53	7.9	7.6	2.4	$96,915,000
Greinke, Zack	92-78	8.9	8.1	2.3	$185,503,000
Lee, Cliff	127-78	8.8	7.4	2.0	$157,855,300
Halladay, Roy	200-102	8	6.9	1.9	$148,991,666

In the history of the game when it comes to the pitchers who have been successful, they all have something in common. Besides having a repeatable delivery that gives them great command of two to four pitches in their repertoire. The most important pitch is the fastball, and they commanded it to both sides of the plate and down. They also threw it above the strike zone and below the zone when necessary. If they threw a curve ball and slider or just one of the two, they can throw it for strikes at the bottom of the zone on any count. They can also back door the curve ball or the slider which means that they can throw it right-handed pitcher to left-handed hitter on the very outside corner of the plate for a strike to freeze a hitter. When it comes out of the pitcher's hand, it looks like a ball, but when the catcher receives it on the corner, it is a strike. The same thing occurs when a left-handed pitcher throws it away to a right-handed batter. They can also do the complete opposite which is called a front door curveball or slider. When a right-handed pitcher throws it to a right-handed hitter in the direction of his front shoulder or rib cage, it hits the inside corner of the strike zone locking up the hitter. The change-up is a pitch that comes in different forms as far as grips are concerned. A few names are the fosh, circle change, and split-finger. They all have the same characteristics, which is designed to look like a fastball, but the grip takes the velocity down 10 to 14 miles per hour less than their fastball making it a change of pace. This is all in place to throw off the hitters timing.

These pitchers are successful because they induce contact early in counts. They work fast between pitches making hitters uncomfortable because they are always in attack mode unless they need to slow the game down. They mix their pitches staying unpredictable especially in hitting counts, which is when they are behind on hitters. We are all human, and make mistakes, but when these pitchers display their abilities to command their pitches, and when they do miss, it is by a small margin.

These elite pitchers in the illustration show their win-loss record, hits, and strikeouts per 9 innings, but the most important category is the bases on balls. Four of the fifteen pitchers listed above had 3 bases on balls per 9 innings pitched and the rest were below. The magic number is 3 bases on balls per 9 innings they pitch in. The way pitchers have a low amount of base on ball is by throwing first-pitch strikes. They work ahead of most hitters unless they are pitching around a hitter to get to another. They put themselves in put away situations often and make hitters chase balls that look like strikes. As I mentioned earlier, they have secondary pitches that they can get over the plate when a hitter is in a fastball count.

These pitchers do all the little things right, all the time. Doing things right is a way of life for them. They pay close attention to detail and they want to be the best in every aspect of the game. They are fearless competitors who believe in themselves and will not back down from any situation. Their work ethic is second to none as a little extra is a common practice.

The most important part of this segment is that these pitchers make a lot of money based on what they have done or do to accomplish these great statistics. Notice how much they have made during their entire careers. Each pitcher comes with his strengths and weaknesses, and not all of them are hard throwers with their fastballs that touch or reach 94 to 97 miles per hour, but they locate their pitches consistently from pitch to pitch, inning to inning, and game to game. They understand the importance of location when it comes to being successful. Pitchers that can command the baseball are considered smart, and pitchers that are hard throwers with no command are not held in that same light. Throughout this book, we will continue to emphasize the importance of command as it trumps everything else.

Greg Maddux was once asked over a friendly teammates' dinner, which was the best game he had ever pitched? They also asked him, was it a no-hitter? He had never thrown a no-hitter. Was it a one-hitter? Etc. To their surprise, his answer was a game in which he located or in his words he hit his spot 102 out of 106 pitches.

CHAPTER 23

Mixing Pitches to Control the Count

Mixing

Pitchers	Fastball	Curve	Slider	Change	Other
Roy Halladay	71.26%	13.22%	0.00%	15.53%	0.00%
Cole Hamels	72.22%	7.32%	0.00%	20.45%	0.00%
Felix Hernandez	57.14%	12.82%	15.02%	15.02%	0.00%
Josh Johnson	61.79%	7.55%	23.58%	7.08%	0.00%
Cliff Lee	77.79%	7.32%	4.36%	10.53%	0.00%
John Lester	74.35%	14.49%	0.00%	11.16%	0.00%
CC Sabathia	62.08%	5.55%	16.99%	15.38%	0.00%
Jered Weaver	54.58%	10.07%	18.95%	16.39%	0.00%

When we see this chart, we see a break down on how each of these elite pitchers mixes his pitches to keep hitters off balance. We are always prioritizing when it comes to command. In order to be an effective pitcher, we must be able to locate two to three pitches for strikes. It is obvious the number one pitch we must learn to locate is the fastball because by doing so, it will allow you to get to your secondary pitches. By observing this chart, we see how important it is for most of these pitchers to throw their change-ups to balance their repertoire. Notice only one pitcher from this group throws the change-up less than 10% of the time with his second-best pitch being the slider. The rest of these pitchers are over that 10% mark because at the highest level it is paramount to get the world's best hitters out. It is important that we throw it at least 10% of the time. Keep in mind that the change-up has the least average against pitch at the Major League level.

We see that four of the eight pitchers threw fastballs over 70% of the time. Roy Halladay is at 71%, and he threw sinkers and cutters, and that is the reason he is over that 70% mark. Cliff Lee is another pitcher who throws two types of fastballs one being a cutter he throws to right-handed hitters often and the other being a four-seam fastball. Cole Hamels is at 72% but complements it with 20% change-ups, and John Lester at 74%. Both Hamels and Lester have tremendous command of their fastballs with late sinking action which is the reason they have so much confidence with it.

Five of these eight pitchers threw four different pitches and are the most balanced with their repertoire. They can throw any pitch on any count making it very difficult to have success against them. That is the beautiful thing about pitching when you have these many pitches that you can throw for strikes, as a pitcher you start to recognize what hitters are trying to do just with their gestures and body movements. Nothing gets a hitter out of his game plan, more than when we attack the zone in quality areas and go back and forth, which is changing speeds and then change eye level. Down below the strike zone and up hands and above. Pitching is an art. Pitchers that locate well are called painters. They are also called surgeons as they can operate on a line-up surgically carving them up.

In closing, we need to always work on throwing all our pitches for strikes. If it becomes a challenge to throw strikes the hitter starts to hunt fastballs, and you become their prey. We should always have the upper hand as hitting is the hardest thing to do in all sports. The best hitters are successful 30% of the time with three hits out of every ten at bats. The odds are in our favor, and we should pitch as such. Going after hitters and mixing your pitches is the key to success.

CHAPTER 24

Control Batter by Controlling the Baseball

Throughout this system, we've emphasized the importance of having good command which is another example of having a systematic chart that can break down a pitch by pitch sequence that gives you positive results for easy outs or negative results that lead to long at-bats, deep counts and ultimately to predictability and base on balls. This chart is the characteristics an at-bat takes based on each pitch. We are always trying to stay on the left side of the chart, which will get us quick and easier outs compared to falling behind batters making it harder to keep them off the bases. As we mentioned in the Cat and Mouse section of this system, hitters are giving us something, and we as pitchers can take advantage to get ahead of them-- a place a hitter does not want to be.

The very first pitch we make is the most important pitch. That's not to say that every pitch isn't important, but it means that when we get ahead of hitters, they start to think and if hitters are thinking it can lead to them getting out of their game plan and that first pitch does a lot to sway at-bats into a pitcher's favor. The other count we keep mentioning is the 1-1 count. This 1-1 count is big in swaying the count because numbers show the biggest difference in the at-bat, is when a pitcher throws a ball or a strike making it 2-1 versus 1-2 put away situation. The plate gets smaller when you get behind hitters, but it expands to around 21 to 22 inches when hitters have two strikes. Getting to two strikes in an at-bat is what we strive for unless the game or your manager tells us it's time to pitch around a hitter and it means a smart base on ball to get a matchup or face a less dangerous hitter in a crucial part of the game. Also, some hitters are notorious or susceptible to swinging at pitches that look like strikes out of your hand but turn out to be balls out of the strike zone. On the other hand, when pitchers start to nibble on the corners of the plate, it is extremely tough to stay ahead of hitters. There's a part of the plate hitters is not looking to hit or make contact early, because if they do it can lead to them getting themselves out and most of the time that is what happens. We as pitchers make a well-located pitch, but if the hitter doesn't recognize it and swings early in an at-bat, they get themselves out. Two things that get hitters out and that is the location of a pitch, and the other is the speed. For example, we can have two strikes on a hitter, and he's looking away and protecting in against fastballs. If we throw him a fastball down and away, he could possibly get to that pitch due to the situation, but if you threw him a change-up, he could be out front and roll over or have an arm swing with no leverage. He can also be looking away with two strikes, and we bust him inside on the black with a fastball and freeze him. The saying is it isn't the pitch; it's how you got there that gets them out.

The illustration below is the chart that navigates a pitcher through an at-bat when facing a hitter. From the very first pitch to the seventh pitch and beyond that either get a hitter out early or prolongs an at-bat that can lead to a base on ball. It gives a pitcher or a coach a good visual, and one sees it from a different standpoint that can drive home and simplify the process.[9]

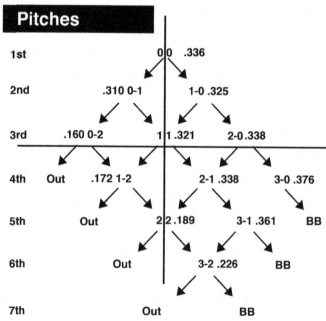

This chart gives you a perfect illustration of what happens after each pitch and how it changes each at-bat from pitch to pitch. Notice at the very top on the first pitch if you throw a strike the average is still .310. Pitchers need to keep the first pitch down at the hitter's knees, and that average drops down to .211 when hitters put the ball in play. If the pitcher throws another strike, the average dramatically goes down to .160. With two strikes hitters are scrambling because they have 7" to 8" inches of sweet spot to work with compared to 17" plus inches the plate becomes, which makes it almost impossible to cover both sides.

When the pitcher throws a chase pitch off the plate and hitter doesn't offer at it, then the count is 1-2 and still in the pitcher's favor. .172 A chase pitch should always set up the next pitch. The objective is to throw a strike on the 1-2 pitch because we want to avoid having a hitter in a 0-2 count and before you know it, the count is 2-2 or 3-2, and now advantage sways back to the hitter. Remember that pitching inside with your fastball is good when having two strikes on hitters. Be aggressive, and your intention should be to get him out on the inside part of the plate, which I call shaving the black.

Hitters do not fear pitchers that cannot throw strikes inside to get them out. They will take the pitch and hit your best offering to the opposite field with ease. Our motto should be to get hitters out on three pitches or less because you are pounding the strike zone and putting them on the defense and most importantly preserve your pitch count. Greg Maddux routinely pitched nine-inning complete games with less than 100 pitches because he was in attack mode in the strike zone. Get ahead, induce early contact and put hitters away when you have the opportunity.

Throwing balls on the first pitch can lead to pitchers having their backs up against the wall. This means that hitters start to hunt fastballs because there are no longer in guessing mode. They can gamble on looking for a fastball in a certain area usually that's middle of the plate and inside. They can put those 7" to 8" of sweet spot to square a pitch up. If we stay on that right side of the chart it leads you to make lots of pitches, running up your pitch count, and that is always good for the hitters. The more pitches they see the easier it is for them to recognize and time your pitches. We need to show that we are competitors with aggressiveness, attack hitters in the strike zone. If we are shying away from contact, it could lead to pitchers losing confidence, and teammates and coaches losing confidence in you as well. At any level of baseball, pitchers end up losing their rolls or job, and at a professional level, pitcher's get demoted and possibly released which is a place that no pitcher wants to be.

CHAPTER 25

Ahead Early Behind

The Ahead Early Behind charting is a great way to teach pitchers how to keep track of what happens when they pitch their way into these separate areas. With this system, coaches can keep track of when hitters reach base from these counts. The counts will be broken down to understand what we're keeping track of exactly. Like I mentioned earlier, it's how many hitters reach base from these counts. We will be tracking On Base.

How do we keep track of the hitters that reach base?

If a pitcher induces contact on any of the Early counts 0-0/0-1/1-0/1-1 you put it on the right of the Early section how many times hitters put the ball in play and on the left if he reached base. Basically, how many times on the right, and how many reach bases on the left.

Once the pitcher gets into the Ahead side of the chart, which is 0-2/1-2, it doesn't matter what happens from that point on. We keep track if the hitter gets on base or not. The only time you do not add a runner is if he reaches on an error. All others that reach base will get counted.

The next counts are when getting Behind on the right side of the chart. 2-0/2-1

Once the pitcher gets into these counts it doesn't matter if the count goes to 3-2 if he gets on base except for an error, it gets counted on the left side as hitter reaching base. After having accumulated enough innings, this becomes a pitcher's report card. If he gets ahead of hitters, but a high number reach base, it simply means he's having trouble finishing off hitters and as a coach you know he needs to improve on the execution of put away combinations.

When a pitcher induces early contact and again a high number is reaching base, it means he's more likely than not, elevating pitches in the strike zone giving hitters good looks for solid contacts early in counts. As his coach, we embrace this by re-enforcing how important it is to pitch at the bottom of the strike zone and making him aware that his ground ball to fly ball ratio must improve, and ground balls usually are much better than fly balls.

When a pitcher is in the behind side, the hitters that reach base is usually off the charts. I do not know of many pitchers who stay in the game very long getting behind in counts to hitters often at whatever level of baseball he pitches in. If he has a high number of getting behind hitters, it usually means that he's not attacking hitters, especially on the 0-0 counts. First pitch strikes are imperative for a pitcher's success. The 1-1 count is the other time we want to stress to our pitchers. On the other hand, if he doesn't get behind often, but has a high number reach base, we take this time to work on better fastball command and or incorporate the Changeups, Curveballs or Sliders for strikes when behind or in fastball counts. This is a great system to bond with your pitchers and educate them on how they can become better performers based on their very own statistics.

The Early counts are	0-0/0-1/1-0/1-1
The Behind counts are	2-0/2-1
The Ahead counts are	0-2/1-2

In a recent study conducted of one of the two leagues at the highest level of baseball, the numbers told this story.

Inducing contact on 0-0/0-1/1-0/1-1
The league studied had a .338 On Base Percentage
The team studied had a .320 On Base Percentage

To a pitcher's benefit, the only time these numbers changed was when his pitches crossed the plate at the bottom of the strike zone, which brought that number down to .211, which also indicated more ground balls and softer contact by hitters.

When it came to these early counts, the 1-1 count is the one that plays a huge impact of swaying the at-bat in the favor of hitter or pitcher. When a pitcher threw a ball on this count, the On Base Percentage ballooned to a league average of .454 making it a just about a 50/50 chance the hitter would reach base. Two teams studied had been below the league average and did not make the playoffs that year.

They had for the year a .464 and .469 OBP. According to the Ahead Early Behind study, two of the elite pitchers had a .314 and .354 OBP. The team in the study had their two best pitchers with a .408 and .417 OBP. If you noticed the four pitchers studied were better than the league average. The reason was that they could throw secondary pitches behind in counts or located the fastball in the money areas of the strike zone. That location is usually down and away to the hitter. The Change-up is a great weapon to have as a pitcher, especially in these counts. It is the least average against pitch at the highest level when having good arm speed without slowing the body down to try and help the velocity. A great WEAPON TO HAVE!

This is the fun part for a pitcher, when he throws a strike on the 1-1 count the OBP league average dramatically dropped to a minuscule .211 OBP. The two elite pitchers studied had a .165 and .177 OBP and the two-team pitchers tracked had a .159 and .198 OBP team best. When elite pitchers get into a put-away count they are masters at making balls look like strikes. They expand the zone by being masters of pitching out of the tunnel. Basically, that's out of their fastball release point not giving hitters information from 60' feet 6" inches forcing them to make late decisions and that's usually around 45' and that in essence is just too late. A pitcher's mentality should be when in this situation, this at-bat is over!

We need to be in both the Ahead and Early counts 70% of the time

Keys to run prevention – Above average Ground to Fly ball ratio

These numbers do not change much from year to year

High rate of swings and misses (Pitching out of the tunnel)

Avg OBP .338 / Good OBP .349 / Grt OBP is .370 (Pitchers .177 OBP)

NOTE: Notice when having hitters in an 0-2 or 1-2 count, it's like you are pitching to a pitcher comparing his normal hitting average.

This system is a great way of getting to know and teaching your pitchers how to become better performers.

In this section, I've provided a sheet I use to keep track of this information and develop a pitcher's report card.[10]

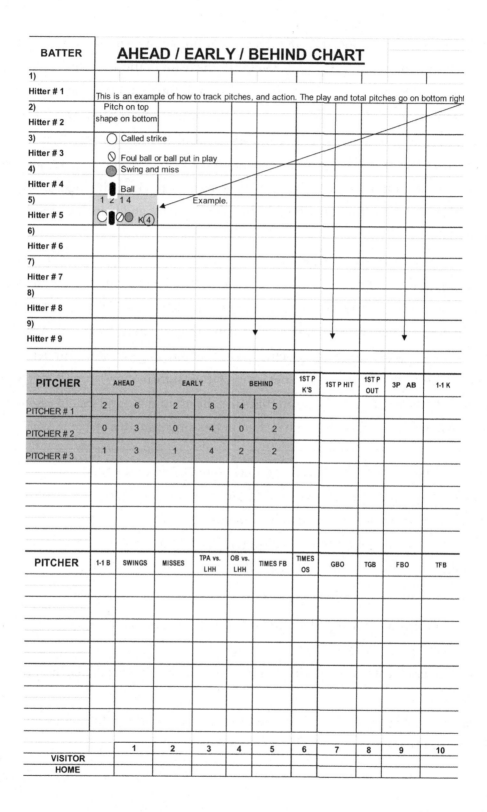

BATTER	AHEAD / EARLY / BEHIND CHART						
1) Hitter # 1	This is an example of how to track pitches, and action. The play and total pitches go on bottom right						
2) Hitter # 2	Pitch on top shape on bottom						
3) Hitter # 3	○ Called strike						
4) Hitter # 4	⊘ Foul ball or ball put in play						
5) Hitter # 5	● Swing and miss						
6) Hitter # 6	▮ Ball						
7) Hitter # 7	1 2 1 4 Example. ○▮⊘● K④						
8) Hitter # 8							
9) Hitter # 9							

PITCHER	AHEAD		EARLY		BEHIND		1ST P K'S	1ST P HIT	1ST P OUT	3P AB	1-1 K
PITCHER # 1	2	6	2	8	4	5					
PITCHER # 2	0	3	0	4	0	2					
PITCHER # 3	1	3	1	4	2	2					

PITCHER	1-1 B	SWINGS	MISSES	TPA vs. LHH	OB vs. LHH	TIMES FB	TIMES OS	GBO	TGB	FBO	TFB

	1	2	3	4	5	6	7	8	9	10
VISITOR										
HOME										

162

CHAPTER 26

MLB Averages by Counts

There's a saying that numbers do not lie. In this section, we have taken the best hitters in the world and have shown you their averages to understand and be aware of what we need to do for success. Understanding the statistics to these counts makes you realize how important it is to get ahead of hitters. In this illustration we notice that when hitters have two strikes against them, they have too many things to think about, making it extremely difficult to hit. If you are a young pitcher trying to get to the next level, your velocity means a lot to you, but when facing good hitters' velocity doesn't mean much to them. They can hit a fastball with velocity if they know it's coming. What makes them uncomfortable is the command of the fastball to both sides of the plate and down as well as mixing secondary pitches for strikes.

It is interesting how every two-strike count has an average of less than .200 except for the 3-2 count, which is .226. The .226 / 3-2 count average is because you might catch too much of the plate to avoid a base on ball. The only count that raises the average above the .200 with two strikes is the 3-2 count making it vitally important, to get ahead with the first pitch, and the 1-1 count as often as we can to avoid making unnecessary pitches that put a pitcher on the defense or eat up your pitch count.

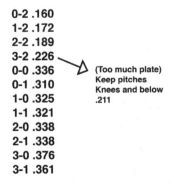

0-2 .160
1-2 .172
2-2 .189
3-2 .226
0-0 .336
0-1 .310
1-0 .325
1-1 .321
2-0 .338
2-1 .338
3-0 .376
3-1 .361

(Too much plate)
Keep pitches
Knees and below
.211

All other counts have an average of over .300 or above. The only time these over .300 averages change is when pitchers pitch at the bottom of the zone, which means at the hitter's knees or below. The number drops to .211. Why? It is because what hitters see is the top half of the ball and when he goes to make contact, he hits what he sees consequently inducing him into hitting the ball on the ground.

Pitches up in the zone can change a game because they hit what they see and that's the back part of the ball. They can sway the game or the score with one swing of the bat. Balls get hit out of the park, off the wall, over an outfielder's head, etc. On the other hand, it's a different story if the ball is put in play on the ground. The saying is, "it takes 3 hits to beat you on the ground, but it only takes one swing of the bat to beat you with a pitch up in the zone."

We must always master a game plan. We keep our thought's organized and in sequential order, to refer to, during the game. Here are some examples of what these thoughts could be.

1. Think of one pitch at a time. Breathing is very important and should be under control to stay cool calm and collected. Good rhythm and tempo will be constant with your pre-pitch routine.

2. Hit the glove. When we think of hitting the glove, try not looking at the whole glove as a target. The great pitchers look inside of the glove picking up a lace or a light coming through the web of the pocket and simply hit it.

3. Each hitter is a separate game. Remember the game is made up of lots of little battles and each hitter represents those battles. If we win most of those battles, we stand a chance to be on the winning end and win the war.

4. Based on the numbers, keep in mind that hitters are good when we get careless up and middle of the strike zone, but if we pitch at the knees and below, they aren't as successful, .211 keep your pitches down.

5. Hitters will try and eliminate something from you. They are trying to eliminate a pitch you are having trouble locating, and they have one less thing to worry about basically backing you up into a corner.

6. Every pitch that comes out of your hand must have a purpose and 100% (CONCENTRATION) on it. We can't emphasize this enough. Focus and concentration are at the heart of the matter for a pitcher.[11]

CHAPTER 27

Control vs. Command

What type of Pitcher are you?

Control

Command

When pitchers see themselves, a question they should ask is what type of pitcher am I? Am I a control or command pitcher? What is the difference between control and command?

It's very important to understand how vital it is for a pitcher to be conscious of his preparation when it comes to the command of his pitches. Young pitchers should realize the importance of focus and concentration he must have when doing all throwing programs with the sole intention of hitting intended targets. We should have a purpose before that ball leaves our hand. Too many young pitchers throw just to throw without the concept of hitting a target. It could be your partner's shoulder, it could be his hip or simply his glove, just have an idea before making the pitch.

The difference between command and control is when a pitcher throws a pitch, he can get it in the strike zone, but he could've been focusing on the outside part of the plate, and it missed to the complete opposite side. He was locating down, but it got away from him and missed with the pitch up. This type of pitcher can be a strike thrower but is not able to be consistent enough to put it in the nine boxes of the strike zone. He can be a competitive pitcher, but usually not a winner.

We keep alluding to command because we cannot emphasize this enough on how important it is to be a consistent pitcher. Good pitchers are definitive on how they go about their business and never take this vital part for granted and or lightly. They are obsessed with being able to make pitches throughout those nine boxes, and they never pass up an opportunity to work on it.

A pitcher is the most important part of a team's designed game plan. If the pitcher locates his pitches, for the most part, his position players will more likely than not be in the right place to defend against opposing hitters. On the other hand, if he doesn't locate his pitches that game plan is just a plan. With the ability to command your pitches, we gain the confidence of our teammates, manager, and coaches.

They know you can be relied on to compete and keep them in ball games giving them a chance to win. No matter what level you're pitching in, the best pitchers throw quality strikes because they command that baseball. I ask you again, what type of pitcher are you? If a pitcher isn't working on being a command pitcher, he is missing the concept of what pitching is. Command pitchers have the most fun on the mound and get paid extremely well.

CHAPTER 28

What Pitchers Want Hitters to Know About Them

When pitchers are facing a line-up, they break down every hitter's strengths and weaknesses. They go over what hitters like to bunt. Which ones like to steal bases and those who the opposing team likes to hit and run with? Then pitchers go into every hitter's statistics. Which hitters like to swing at the first pitch and what are the statistics of every count they hit in. Are they pull hitters or like to go the other way? Who are the more disciplined hitters? What hitter is susceptible at chasing pitches out of the zone? With runners on bases, does the hitter have lower averages or higher and does he hit behind the runners well in different situations. All this information allows a pitcher to formulate a game plan. Now that a pitcher has gotten himself ready mentally to execute his game plan, he goes into concentration mode and gets the job done.

Now that a pitcher has a thorough profile of the hitters, the big question is what does the scouting report say about us? The same holds for how hitters perceive pitcher's strengths and weaknesses, scouting reports, and strategies and overall tendencies. After researching all the information on profiling a pitcher or a hitter, then the psychological warfare process begins.

We want hitters to have a tough time knowing they will not get much to hit even though you are a pitcher who attacks the zone. Let's go a little further into this and find out how to keep hitters always on their toes. Remember velocity with poor command is a recipe for failure.

The first question you want him to know about you is:

- Can this pitcher locate his fastball to both sides and down at the bottom of the strike zone, which is at the hitter's knees and below?

- Can this pitcher throw a change-up for strikes and to both sides of the plate?

- Can he locate his curveball or slider or both for strikes on any count?

- Can this pitcher expand the strike zone for put-away pitches by making balls look like strikes?

- Can he back door and front door his off-speed pitches for strikes?

- Can he throw his fastball in for strikes to get the hitter out and in off the plate for effect or intimidate? (Gets hitter off game plan)

- When a pitcher's efficiency becomes this good, the hitter says to himself, "Wow! I must wait him out until he makes a mistake," as per Mark McGuire.

When hitters step up to the plate, they have certain things on their mind. One of those things that are very important to them is they want to eliminate pitches from a pitcher's repertoire, therefore allow me to share a couple of situations that you may face in games.

If a pitcher is a nibbler which means a pitcher who doesn't attack the strike zone because he lives on the edges, the hitter allows for the pitcher to get behind in the count for them to hunt that fastball --predictability.

If a left-handed hitter is facing a left-handed pitcher and the pitcher doesn't throw a change-up to lefties, then he eliminates that pitch zeroing on two pitches and if he can't locate that secondary pitch for strikes, then he's backed the pitcher into a corner with only having the ability to throw one pitch.

Pitchers that do not like to throw inside for effect or strikes with their fastball make it difficult on themselves because when a pitcher throws strikes on both sides of the plate, they open many options. On the other hand, if a pitcher pitches on just the outside part of the plate he allows the hitter to eliminate the inside part of the plate from him and can put 7" to 8" of the sweet spot for solid contact.

We as pitchers want to keep as many options open as possible, and the more we do with our pitches, the more difficult we make it on the hitters. As you can see the hitter's job is to take as much as he can from us to back us into a point of vulnerability or predictability. The least we can do with the baseball, the easier it is for them to hit. By having the ability to do so much with the baseball, we challenge the hitter by maneuvering them into a guessing game. Therefore, a pitcher pays attention to detail and couples that with preparation to give himself the best chances to succeed.

CHAPTER 29

Breaking Down A Line-up

Breaking down a line-up is a vital part of pitching. When facing a team, we must learn how to dissect a line-up with the strengths and weaknesses of each hitter. At the professional level, Major League pitchers have videos they can go over, of their appearances against the hitters they're facing. They also have every statistic imaginable from every count or game situations each hitter has faced. They get a good idea of who does what and when they like to do it, as well as knowing the hitter's deficiencies. They also have a team game plan on how to pitch and try to get each hitter out. At the younger levels, the video systems in place have improved dramatically, and with a video person on staff who can give anyone from coaches to individual players whatever information they want. Your coaches are a valuable source. With the information age, a lot of these teams you're playing against have a website with players statistics to get an idea of who is their better hitters. Another way is to simply watch them take batting practice before a game if it's your last resort. We must find a way to prepare ourselves the best way we can.

The game of baseball is in another transitional period now. In the past, the game relied on speed and small ball to put runs on the board. The game of baseball was about speed wrapped around a game swaying swing of the bat in the late 1970s, 80s, and early 90s. Runners would create havoc on the base paths and get pitchers to speed up and induce them into making mistakes to hitters. Also, catchers would call lots of fastballs making it easier to hit with runners on bases. The on base percentage and home runs have changed the game in this new analytics era.

This section is to give you an idea of the characteristics and strengths and weaknesses of each hitter. We broke it down to help make you aware of what to pay attention to and be one step ahead as you are making in-game decisions. Winning pitchers' preparation is second to none; they know the importance of doing their homework before they toe the rubber to compete. They make sure if they get beat, it's because they were outpitched not because they weren't prepared.

As MLB teams take more of an analytical route for their lineup construction, some managers have made the decision to opt for a slightly different approach with their best hitter. The Angels and Yankees opt to put Mike Trout and Aaron Judge respectively in the 2nd position in the lineup as their analytics departments believe that it will help the teams produce more runs. What follows is a more traditional description for how lineups are constructed.

#1 HITTER

- Speed: steals bases
- Patient: takes pitches
- Bunts
- Might have power

#2 HITTER

- Handles bat well; might hit and run
- Takes pitches to allow leadoff hitter to steal
- Sacrifices at-bat for the sake of the team
- Hits behind the runner well

#3 HITTER

- Usually the best hitter in the lineup
- Uses the whole field
- RBI guy
- Possibly runs well
- Possibly a power hitter

Good two-strike approach

APPROACH

- They want to see your best stuff (SEE IF THEY CAN ELIMINATE PITCHES)
- They want to find out your out pitch
- If you can retire each of these first three hitters on 3 pitches or
- less, you are doing great
- You would like to break up the lineup so that the #3 or #4 hitters end an inning or leadoff an inning with no runners on base
- Be prepared to face their 4th batter of the line-up in the 1st inning focusing on making quality pitchers

#4 HITTER

- Power hitter
- Aggressive- possibly strikes out a lot
- Sometimes will be a strictly pull hitter
- RBI guy

#5 HITTER

- Should be a good hitter; if not, the #4 hitter will not get pitches to hit
- RBI guy
- Possibly a gap to gap guy
- Should not strike out a lot
- Still a very dangerous hitter

#6 HITTER

- Power hitter
- RBI guy
- Potentially a disciplined hitter

APPROACH

- These hitters may not have seen the out pitch prior to their first at-bat.
- They are not coming up to see you pitch; they are coming to hack and change the game with one swing of the bat.
- Locate, locate, locate. Make them hit your pitch. Do not lose your aggressiveness as a pitcher.
- You will potentially face 7 batters in the first two innings.

#7 HITTER

- Poor hitter in most cases.
- Lacks discipline.
- Usually has a wider strike zone.
- Lots of holes in his swing.

#8 HITTER

- Reason he is in the lineup- probably a good glove guy.
- Several holes in his swing.

#9 HITTER

- Possibly a patient hitter who works the count.
- Possibly a fast runner who could steal bases.
- Might be a second leadoff type hitter.
- Also, could be the completely opposite-be a terrible hitter.

APPROACH

- Focus on not wasting pitches to this part of the lineup because you will need the pitches when you face the middle of the lineup next time around the order.
- Stay aggressive. Do not lose focus. Continue to make pitches. Do not let your guard down and relax. It could lead you into trouble when the lineup turns over.

CHAPTER 30

Breaking Down Hitters Tendencies

One of the arts a pitcher needs to develop is the ability to recognize a hitter's tendencies. There are characteristics of hitters just by the way they hold the bat and stand at the plate that indicates what type of hitter they are. When a pitcher has mastered the ability to command the baseball and execute a game plan, he then will expand his knowledge to see things that without command, he would not be able to pick up.

In this segment, we will cover what things to look for when breaking down a hitter and his characteristics. We will also cover what pitches to throw once you've seen where the bat is at the point of contact and which pitch you might want to think about throwing once you've gathered that information. It is very informative knowing just by watching how a hitter stands and holds his bat that will lead to a pitcher attacking the strike zone and the sequences he needs to do to get him out.

Visual recognition of Hitters

Flat bat   High-ball hitter
Upright bat   Low-ball hitter
Crouched hitter   High-ball hitter
Hitter who stands tall   Low ball hitter
Hitter who wraps   Pitch Inside
Head movement up/down   Breaking balls

Head movement forward	Change-up
Stands away from plate	Pitch inside
Stands on plate	Pitch away

Hitters Stride

If he dives in	Hard and inside
If he bails out	Soft and away
If he strides straight	Mix pitches away and inside

Stance

If he's open	Pitch away
If he's closed	Pitch him inside

These are just some tips and advice on what to either throw these hitters or what they like to do based on how they hold their bats and stand in the box. When a pull hitter steps up to the plate, pitchers should have in mind what are the pitches that allow this type of hitter to have success. We will mention the ones the pitcher should be able to execute to get them out. The money pitch in baseball is the fastball down and away for the most part. To keep control of the outside part of the plate we need to pitch inside occasionally to keep hitters honest and keep them from sitting on that outside location. When hitters are ahead in a fastball count, they are usually looking to pull the ball. A curveball or slider is also a good pitch to throw in that same area of the strike zone. A change-up is great on pull hitters as well inducing him to be an arm swing hitter, because once he gauges your fastball, he swings at the fastball, but change up comes in 10 to 14 miles an hour slower causing him to lose all his leverage.

When a hitter stands on top of plate meaning in and close to it, he has quick hands and likes to pull the ball in general. He is challenging you to pitch inside. Down and away to this hitter is the location to go and mix secondary pitches to 'keep him off balance. The objective is to use his quick hands against him.

When a hitter stands away from the plate, it usually means that he gets tied up on fastballs inside. He needs to get extended and by standing away from the plate he can get to that inside pitch. This type of hitter should be challenged to the inside part of the plate. Inside is where you want to start until he proves he can get to that pitch. These hitters like the pitch middle of the plate and away. Also, mix your secondary pitches to keep him off balance.

We as pitchers should be aware that a hitter takes his swing with him no matter when he stands on the batter's box. An example is if he's at the back of the batter's box and has trouble with curveball it doesn't matter if he moves up to the front of the box the swing is the same. The only difference is that he's hoping you hang one of those curveballs to hit it before it starts its downward break. He is telling himself, I'm going to hit it in its apex as opposed to the bottom, so scooting up in the box will give him a chance and we counter his thought by keeping it at the knees or below.

When we see a hitter that has an uppercut swing, he usually has a hole, up and in with fastballs in that location. Up and in is usually the tough location on this type of hitter because the bat is dragging through the strike zone. Players on occasions say that this type of hitter has a Swiss cheese swing. The reason is that his front elbow immediately goes up causing his back shoulder and elbow to drop and begin swing upward as appose to down and through the ball level type of swing.

As a rule, avoid the hitter's strength and pitch to his weakness. But, if his strength matches up with your pitcher's strength, choose your pitchers strength. Don't stray from your pitcher's strength to attack the hitter's weakness, especially if it's a pitch the pitcher doesn't throw very well.

Reading swings is the most immediate way to detect a hitter's strengths and weakness. His swing will tell you how to pitch him. Also, by continually reading swings, you can see if a hitter is swinging differently than his scouting report says. You can recognize his changes and make your own adjustments accordingly.

- Timing: Is the hitter early, late or on time at the point of contact?
- If he's late, stay hard on him.
- If he's early, stay soft.

- Which direction does he hit the ball?
- If he's a pull hitter, pitch him soft and away.
- If he's an opposite-field hitter, pitch him hard and inside.
- Plate coverage: Can he cover the inside part of the plate or the outside?
- Attack the side that he's weaker on.
- Expand off the side that he covers well.
- Height: Does he handle the high pitch or low pitch better?

Remembering pitch sequences; a pitcher's mind should work like a Rolodex in relation to each hitter of the lineup he's facing. Remembering each, and every pitch and how you start, get to the middle, and finish hitters should come as second nature with the more experience a pitcher gets. This is what makes competing so much fun when mentally you can be prepared for whatever the games bring at you. They say the game of baseball is a game of inches or sometimes the ball doesn't bounce your way, but when you are prepared the inches and ball bouncing have more of a chance to be in your favor.

- Remember the "action" pitch and the result of a hitter's at-bat.
- What pitch (and location) did he put the ball in play?
- Where and how hard did he hit it?

What was the result?

If he struck out, what pitch (and location) was he unable to put into play?
Remember the sequence of pitches it took to get to the action pitch.

- What pitch did you start him off with?
- What pitches in the middle of the sequence led up to the action pitch?
- What was the action pitch?

A word of advice to pitchers is to carry around a notebook and keep at-bats of opposing hitters describing pitch sequences. How you started them off and what pitches got you to induce him into putting the ball in play or swung and miss. Did the hitter have a different approach with runners on base or in scoring position? Was the hitter overly aggressive with runners on base as appose to when there wasn't? Does he swing at the first pitch? And is the hitter more patient with no runners on base?

Stick to a simple plan.

Throw 1st pitch strikes and 2 of the first 3 pitches for strikes to put yourself in a 1-2 count as often as possible. Doing it with 2 different pitches in vital.

Times a hitter is vulnerable on the inside part of the plate is when the pitcher has 0-1, 0-2, or 1-2, 2-2 counts on the hitter.

Stay on top of throwing as many strikes as you can on the 1-1 count. There is a huge disparity between a pitcher being in a 1-2 count versus a 2-1 count.

Here are examples of four ways to finish off a hitter.

Hard fastball/or off speed

Tilting two pitches in combination (fastball in / Curveball or slider away)

Reverse tilt (Curveball or slider away, Fastball in / Change up away, Fastball up and in)

Doubling up (Fastball in, Fastball in / Fastball away / Fastball away)

Keep in mind that 3 pitches at the same speed and location are extremely dangerous unless exposing a weakness.

Up and away fastballs are easy for a hitter to hit because he can extend his hands and it's easier for him to see the baseball and hit it in a put away situation.

There is no such thing as a wasted pitch. Every pitch sets up the next pitch. An example is when having a 0-2 count and the pitcher throws a curveball or slider in the dirt, the objective is to get hitter diving to the outside part because he must protect every inch of the plate. If you've accomplished him diving, then he's set up for a fastball inside on the black of the plate for a freeze strikeout, broken bat jam shot or swing and miss.

A couple of more examples are to get hitters out.

In-in-out / out-out-in / down-down-up / soft-soft-hard / hard-hard-soft

It is very difficult for a hitter to cover both sides of the plate. If you lead him one way, you can finish him off a different way.

CHAPTER 31

Situational Pitching

Situational pitching will be executed when a pitcher has a good command of his pitches. The games played at the highest level run smoothly when a pitcher can command their pitches in order to execute the game plan. Watch for pitchers getting off to slow starts in the 1st inning. That is the inning in which pitchers are trying to find their rhythm and tempo. Maybe they warm up in the wind up first then stretch, and they start the game the way they started their warm-ups, which was from the wind-up. It can take them an inning to adjust to wind-up again and by that time a crooked number of runs could be on the board. Pitching to the first 3 hitters to end the warm- up routine can help a pitcher that gets off to slow starts.

Pitchers should be aware that one of the offensive numbers that do not go down is the category of the Runs Batted In. Hitters are aware of this category, which at the Major League Level they get paid a king's ransom. Driving runners in from scoring position is vital, and it is one of the statistics that is used to evaluate and assess a hitter. Because of that fact, something happens to hitters mentally when runners are in scoring position; many hitters get over anxious and start to swing at pitches that are not even close to the strike zone early in counts to get themselves into a two-strike situation without even seeing a strike. Why does this happen? They want to drive those runners in so bad that they disconnect mentally and physically and start swinging at pitches they would under normal circumstances just spit on--meaning they would take the pitch with ease and under control. This is an advantage for the pitcher if he's in tune and understands the pressure hitters put themselves in and can exploit it. If he does, he can come out on top in these situations. The tighter the game, meaning tie score or up by one or down by one- the more hitter is susceptible to succumbing to the situation due to self-imposed pressure. So, it starts to reason with runners on 2nd and 3rd or on 3rd and 1 out, in tight game avoid giving up easy runs by giving hitter a cookie when he usually is over anxious and in swing mode to get the RBI, so he expands his strike zone and swings at off-speed pitches chasing them. If you walk him, 1st base is open, and the double play is to get you out of the inning with the pitcher's best friend. When lhp's come out of the pen, it's usually to face a lhh or to turn a switch hitter around to the right side of the batter's box. We should be good at throwing a first pitch-breaking ball for a strike, as hitters are usually sitting on fb's. Walks and errors get teams back into games or expand their leads. When a batter is fouling off all your pitches, go below the zone and see if he chases a pitch down that he sees in his tunnel, below his perception or just hold the ball longer until a thought enters his mind to throw off his timing.

When a left-handed hitter is up with a runner on 1st and no outs or 1 out and even 2 outs in a close game, hitters are taught to pull hitting that 3-4 hole.

1st bsm is on the bag, and 2nd bsm is cheating closer to the bag for a double play. They want to create a 1st and 3rd situation.

We need to learn how to throw off-speed pitches behind in the count when hitters are in swing mode hunting fb's. Or be able to spot a fb in the money spot which is down and away--the big key is DOWN and away in fb counts.

With a runner on 2nd and no outs, the hitter is usually going the other way. Whether it's to just try and advance the runner over or drive him in. They are usually trying to use the big part of the park. Money lies in the RBI'S so, pull hitters get themselves out and do not get RBI's or get the job done in fundamental team offense.

The same thing happens with a runner on 3rd and no outs. The hitter is looking for something up in the zone to get a sacrifice fly to score runner easily. Good time to pitch inside with fb and take the field away from him. Location is black of the plate to off inside towards hitter if we miss. Predictability and elevated pitches are a recipe for failure in this situation. Fastballs up are detrimental to pitchers because a jam shot can get over the infielders' heads or fly balls can score runners from 3rd.

PROTECTING LEADS DEFENSIVELY

Late in the game with the tying or go-ahead run at the plate, the manager will have his 3rd bsm and 1st bsm or one of them guard the lines depending on the hitter to prevent a one swing double on the ground down the lines. The objective is to make them get 3 hits to beat you. It takes five ways to give up extra bases when a pitcher allows contact in the air versus only two on the ground. The two lines and the two gaps equal 4, plus when a ball is hit over the outfielder's head which includes home runs over the fence. Down the lines on the ground are the only two ways to give up extra base hits. The outfielders are usually back at no doubles' depth, which is close to the fence not allowing a fly ball to get over the outfielder's head unless it hits off the wall. This approach logically speaking should be reserved for the 3rd, 4th, 5th, and even 6th hitters that have power versus the hitters who don't drive the ball.

A smart base on ball is when 1st base is open late in close games. Especially with a good hitter up and opposite batter *rhp vs lhh* or *lhp vs rhh* to have the percentages be in your favor match up with the hitter on deck. Early in a game with runner on 1st, outfielders can be positioned further back preventing a runner on 1st from scoring easily. This can apply in a close game all 9 innings. When to play the infield in or halfway with the runner on 3rd?

Example: With a runner on 3rd from the 3rd or 4th inning on and behind in a game by 1 run or ahead by 1 run, which can cost you 2 runs if they get a hit. The manager will more likely than not play with the infielders in. A pitcher is trying to keep the ball on the ground to give infielders a chance to cut down a runner at home. With one out they go on contact with the infield in forcing infielders to make a play at the plate.

CHAPTER 32

Mental Side of Baseball

My first experience with the mental side of baseball came when I was in winter ball during the 1990-1991 Puerto Rican Winter League season when I was pitching for the San Juan Metros. I was having a conversation with a teammate by the name of Reggie Ritter during batting practice. Reggie was the first person who spoke to me about the intricacies of the mental part of the game. The first thing he asked me was what did I see when I looked at the catcher's mitt? I answered, "the mitt." Reggie went on to say that the best pitchers in the game do not see the catcher's mitt, they see a small part inside the glove, like a lace or a light coming through the pocket of the glove and hit it with the pitch. That was how these top pitchers' concentration was at an all-time high.

Reggie mentioned that this was the way these pitchers went about their business on the mound going pitch to pitch. Next, he had me practice a flat ground-throwing program to concentrate on a small piece of the glove and focus on hitting that spot with my fastball. Once I started to get comfortable focusing on that little spot it was amazing how the command of my fastball improved instantly. I was a strike thrower, but not a great command type of pitcher. He continued to challenge me with the drills. Next, he asked to take the same approach, but this time we were going to do it with my secondary pitches. I began throwing the curveball, and he asked me to try and hit the glove every time, and I did just that. It didn't matter where he placed the glove; I was so deep into focusing on that little spot, it became difficult to miss it. What was going on? Reggie had taken my complete focus from over throwing to precise pitching by just focusing on hitting that tiny little spot. We went on to do it with the changeup as well. Every pitch I was making I kept hitting that glove. The logic behind it was aim small, miss small. He also explained to me that the count didn't matter when it came time to make a pitch because the pitch is made when you simply hit the glove.

Once he broke this system down to me, I couldn't wait to get to the park to work on it every day. My favorite phase of our workout became batting practice. During batting practice, I would look forward to learning something new from Reggie. It got to the point in which I would do my flat ground pitching at 50 feet and the batting practice sounds of balls being hit, balls being caught or simple chatter, became almost non-existent. He would shout out a count let's say a 2-2 count on the batter, and he would say it's 2-2, but avoid giving the count any thought, just hit the glove and I would. I could see that Reggie kept getting excited cause the better I became, the more information he wanted to throw at me.

One of the days we had finished practicing he told me that I had to go and buy a sports psychology book titled, *The Inner Game of Tennis*. I had to buy and read it in its entirety. We were not to speak or have conversations as far as pitching was concerned until I was finished with the book. He mentioned to me that he would know if I was finished, by just asking me simple questions. When he quizzed me, I had the answer to each, and every one of them. He felt it was time to move on to other mental areas of pitching.

The Inner Game of Tennis taught me to understand how my mind would get in the way of performing on the baseball field if I allowed it to. How it could work for me or against me, and how to distinguish between the two. The book gave me many examples on what happens when the mind starts to give the body instructions and by doing so, the mind and body were on two different wave links and would be in a fight with each other as opposed to working together as one.

Quieting the mind was the thing I most took away from this book, and it allowed me to pitch at a personal level I had not pitched before. I was pitching at a high level of baseball facing many Major League hitters who were on each of these Puerto Rican Winter League teams with success. I became engaged with making one pitch at a time, and each one of those pitches was just as important as the next. Hitting the glove in games became as easy as when I was hitting Reggie's glove in the outfield during batting practice in our flat ground routine.

I was going through line-ups and recording quick outs because my mistakes were dramatically reduced by getting ahead of hitters in quality areas of the strike zone. I was pitching from the shoulders up using the mind with fluidity. Even though I had been in professional baseball for years, this was something new. Sports psychology seemed to be coming to the forefront of baseball around this time that Reggie brought it to my attention. The game like the saying goes is 90% mental and the other 10% physical.

Reggie felt it was time to teach me a very important part of profound concentration. He began to talk about having a pre-pitch routine. I hadn't the slightest idea what Reggie was talking about, but I gained so much confidence in what he was teaching me that I was all in for the next phase. He shared with me that a pitch isn't made as you release the baseball; it was when you caught the ball back from the catcher. Once you caught the baseball on the mound, the pitch I was about to make had already mentally started. What he meant was that the concentration on the next pitch started once you caught the ball and now would begin a set of steps to narrow your focus.

The three-step drop had already been done. What is a three-step drop? A three-step drop is once you've made the pitch and land with your power leg, that same foot the pitcher lands with he basically walks backward towards the rubber on the mound. It takes three backward steps to get back on the rubber. Once you've done that, the pitcher should be on top of the rubber receiving the ball from the catcher. It keeps the game moving quickly and smoothly having your defense on their toes ready to make plays behind you.

Once you've received the ball, the pitcher looks at the dirt in front of the rubber, focusing on a pebble in the dirt followed by picking up the grass in front of the mound area, and focusing on a blade versus the entire sea of grass. Then track your sight to the dirt in front of the plate, then the catcher's shoes, signs, and location, and then execute the pitch.

This will be your routine from pitch to pitch. It will also help the pitcher's rhythm and timing. It reminded me of a basketball player on the foul line ready to make a free throw. He bounces the ball several times tracks the parquet floor with his eyes and then looks up at the basket to make the shot. Meanwhile, the fans are going crazy behind the basket to distract him, but he is in a zone with nothing but the basket in his sights.

I began to use these lessons in games with my pitching. I found myself so focused I wasn't aware of anything outside of the white lines. With the ability to be so focused I began to see things I wasn't aware of before. I started to recognize hitter's point of contact, which in turn helped me with my pitch selection. I noticed that if I missed the glove it wasn't by much with anyone of my pitches. I could throw three pitches for strikes before, but now I was throwing three pitches with command, which is another level of pitching.

This all culminated when I was summoned to pitch with runners on second and third against Caguas and no outs in the top of the tenth inning in a tied game. I was in a zone seeing Junior Ortiz catcher's mitt look so big that I couldn't miss it and eventually struck out the side with fans erupting into a deafening ovation of joy and euphoria. Before I struck out the last batter of that inning, I did not hear or see anyone or anything but that catcher's mitt.

In the 1990-1991 championship series for the Puerto Rican Winter League title, I pitched 12 scoreless innings and was named Co-MVP along with Hector Villanueva as we won and represented Puerto Rico in the Caribbean Series in Miami, Florida. I owe it to the introduction of the Mental Side of Baseball, as for the first time in my career I was privy to it, and it changed the way I played the game from that point on.

It is highly recommended that as a pitcher one takes the time to sort out materials in this field. The sooner a pitcher becomes aware and strives to embrace this side of the game the more you will develop mentally and once a pitcher has developed the fundamental skills the game becomes a mental battle against the opposition.

There are many sports psychology books that can help you become in tune with the mental side of the game. Major League Clubs have a Sports psychologist to work with their Big Leaguers as well as the Minor League players. It is a vital part of the game that pitchers need to explore and find a way to make it part of the routine.

Getting to understand how the mind works from preparation to competition and from talent to performance lies in the mind of an athlete. To be able to do all your routines with profound concentration focusing on technique when you're working with a trainer. Working on form and technique when doing your conditioning program and even when working on your delivery, they all require you to focus and concentrate at a deep level, which trickles into your game when competing. Striving for excellence starts in the mind and works its way out.

Many outside interferences can cause a player to lose focus. The things that affect a player become distractions. Distractions come from many different directions that can blindside a player. Losing a loved one, an immediate family member becoming very ill, a break up in a relationship, a partying lifestyle, and substance abuse are some of the life challenges that players face.

Players are like everyone else, human. Players are not excluded from normal life experiences. It's how we handle these situations that will allow players to perform well or just take a step and time away from the game to center yourself. A sports psychologist steps into these players' difficult situations in order to get them through tough times. They work on explaining what's going on and the steps needed to take for them to be able to compete as well as handle their personal adversities.

Today, technology can get in the way of focus and concentration. The cell phone is the one that stands at the top of the list. Coming in second is video games that also come in cell phones. A player can have his own personal rules. Once he gets to the park, he can turn off his phone 30 minutes prior to the game. The exception is an emergency, in which case, a point person can be reached during a game.

When young pitchers play at the amateur levels from little leagues on through High school and some cases colleges, they play on raw ability. They dominate the competition and do not have to think much as they can get by mostly on talent alone. Once they reach most of the best colleges and professional baseball, the mind must be utilized with talent. By using his mind, a pitcher is in the process of turning his talents into a skill, which become very valuable for a scholarship or a professional contract. The saying that talent can only get you, but so far, is true because it's up to the mind to get you the rest of the way.

Once a pitcher has developed the mental side into his game the step that follows is mental toughness. Mental toughness is the time invested on the mental side that when a pitcher is performing under pressure, he can apply the psychological lessons he's learned to stay cool, calm, and collected when it's most required of him to make a pitch. Does the pitcher study film of the opposing team to see the strength and weaknesses that as a pitcher can be exposed to his advantage in games? Does he know the numbers, which indicates what hitters do in certain counts and what is the hitters walk to strikeout ratio? Does the pitcher work on the powerful tool of visualizing?

A pitcher can go through a line-up and make pitch after pitch with his eyes closed without ever throwing one pitch. It's like seeing yourself make pitches for a whole or parts of a game; then once you do it in the live situation, it's like déjà vu, he's been there before. **The mind doesn't feel the difference between visualizing and reality.** It's like when we awake from a dream; we think it was happening in real life.

A pitcher can visualize his bullpens sessions, his games, flat ground throwing, pitching in the World Series, etc. Visualization is one of the most overlooked tools a professional athlete can use to take himself to the next level of performance. If a sports psychologist doesn't suggest visualization techniques, it usually isn't going to be practiced, except for a selective group.

There's usually only one sports psychologist per organization in professional baseball. A pitcher can do his due diligence to inquire and take ownership of the mental side of baseball. When the time comes that you can sit down with a sports psychologist you can understand what he is trying to convey to you. The pitcher will receive the information with the right frame of mind to improve and take his pitching to the next level.

Mental toughness pays pitcher's big dividends on those days when we aren't feeling 100%. As a pitcher, we are not going to be in sync every game, and that is very challenging to a young pitcher. The word panic can set in, and it affects a pitcher by having some sort of anxiety. When anxiety sets in, a pitcher will start to experience shortness of breath, which lead to tightening of the muscles and can become a pitcher that isn't functioning at his best on that given game.

Being mentally tough gives a pitcher the ability to stay focused and concentrate on his game plan, but that plan requires one to stay in control of emotions and more importantly your breathing. Breathing is the beginning of it all. Getting control of your breathing is the first area sports psychologist talk about and applying it when a pitcher is competing.

If a pitcher is experiencing nervousness in games the therapist will have the pitcher practice breathing in and out very slowly, so a pitcher can apply this technique when he's starting to encounter anxiety on the field. Breathing will get a pitcher to go through the process of pressure and get back on track with the game plan and execution of pitches to guide or like a GPS, get you to your destination, which is to make the quality pitches necessary, to get out of a tough situation in a game.

The game of baseball isn't a sprint; it's more like a marathon. In the Major Leagues, their schedule covers 162 games. At the minor league level, they play 140 games. College baseball programs start practicing in January, and after the season players go on to play in a league throughout the summer and then come back to a fall program at school. Younger players play in leagues throughout the year in warm weather states.

In the cold weather states or countries, indoor facilities are packed with players working on improving their skills all winter long. When getting to a clubhouse, a stadium, or a ball field a player is required to turn on his mental switch to map out what he's going to improve in on that given workout or practice. When turning on that mental switch a player can prioritize and put his workout into perspective. Setting goals for your practice are excellent to get it done.

Checking your ego at the door and getting down to business is the start. A player doesn't have time to waste to get better in every workout, practice, or game. Focus and concentration, as well as time management, are vital to acquire psychological strength. Little by little, day in and day out, when an athlete takes on this approach, he will be hard to beat.

In many cases it isn't the most talented player that succeeds, it's the low round draft pick or that non-drafted free agent that gets to the major leagues because of his mental toughness. They do not accept anything less than the best of themselves as they take advantage of every second, minute, hour, day, weeks, months, and years that they are in the game. The older an athlete is, the more important this Mental Toughness area becomes because they are trying to squeeze out every bit of ability and talent, they have left to get another pay day.

Many pitchers waste mental energy on unnecessary things they cannot control. They are realizing that the only thing you can control is yourself and how you make a pitch. Once that pitch has left your hand you've lost control of what is about to happen. An umpire can miss a called strike, an infielder can make an error on a routine play, an outfielder can drop a fly ball, the batter can break his bat, and the ball goes just over the infielder's head for a hit. There are so many things that the game of baseball will challenge you with, that unless the pitcher learns to accept and stay within himself when these challenges arise, he will be going against the current.

Can a pitcher just see the new situation and go through his pre-pitch routine focus and concentrate on executing a pitch that will get him out of any difficult situation he finds himself? It all goes back to mental toughness.

My coaching career has covered 22 years and until this day I research the mental side of the game constantly. At the professional level, it is a vital piece of the puzzle and the higher the level, the more important it becomes. There is so much information thrown at a professional player that he must have the mental discipline to take it all in and decipher which he will use and make it part of his DNA of his game.

I love teaching the intricacies of the game, which covers the gamut, but none more important than being mentally strong. Breaking down the pie in the mental area of the game is one of the foundations for professional athletes, and one should take great pride in having a player go deep down inside and muster the necessary time and effort not to overlook this part of his game. It is without a doubt that the best performers on a baseball diamond are the mentally strong players who stay within themselves and execute the game plan.

When I think back at the time I was in my zone and pitching my best baseball games, I was engaged in the moment of every pitch. I was so deep into focus and concentration that all my senses were enhanced and at another level. The catcher's mitt seemed to be so big, that if I missed, it would still be within the glove. The game was so much easier even though it was at a high level it was all because of the mental flow I was experiencing. The success was all made possible by a simple conversation with a teammate that allowed me to experience what the professional game of baseball was all about.

CHAPTER 33

What Goes Through A Pitchers Mind (Confidence or Lacking it)?

THE UNSUCCESSFUL PITCHER

THE SUCCESSFUL PITCHER

In baseball, all players go through a dark side and pitchers are not exempted from this place of despair. Going into this place is called losing confidence. When this happens to a pitcher, there is self-doubt which leads him slowly into an abyss. This place starts in the pitcher's mind, and it works its way through his central nervous system which ultimately attacks the muscles by becoming tight to the point that the body doesn't function at its athletic norm which can be called paralysis by analysis. Slowly a pitcher starts to change what made him successful because he's lost trust and convinces himself that by tinkering here and tinkering there, will get different results. He does not realize that he's taking himself further from his natural abilities and now he is stuck in no man's land.

The mind is the most powerful tool in the body. The mind can take you to the heights and the pinnacle of your dreams. On the other hand, it can lead to your demise by being too analytical. When your thoughts become segmented, and you no longer are in a flow of the mind, body, and soul, a pitcher is apprehensive about competing. How does the pitcher get to the euphoric state of being in a zone? What are the thoughts that go through a pitcher's mind when they start to question themselves?

First and foremost, they become tense. There is a difference between being intense and tense. If you take the I N of intense, we pinpoint the initial place where a pitcher's problems begin. Being loose and feeling as one with the mind and body is the start. When a pitcher tightens up with his muscles, he starts to force things to happen, and nothing good happens when this occurs.

He may start to think about his mechanics. If a pitcher starts to think about his mechanics, he will have difficulty making pitches. His thoughts should be in tune with his hand-eye coordination-- not mechanics-- to flow from pitch to pitch. A pitcher can talk himself into making mistakes on the mound by thinking I can't walk this guy, or I can't hang this pitch, etc. Before you know it, he does what he said he shouldn't do. Another thought that might cross his mind is simply giving hitters too much credit.

When this happens, he'll leave a pitch up in the zone for a hitter to square it up and hit it solidly. If this becomes his thinking, he will succumb to the situation, and he will usually be in the locker room or the showers calling it an early night.

When a pitcher has come to terms with reaching this bottomless pit, what does he need to do to climb out of this rut? Where is the start or the beginning stages of turning this around? The answer is in the 3 C's. The 3 C's are always in effect, and most pitchers are using them on normal bases without thinking about them. However, when a pitcher is in his low point with confidence, we go back to the basics of the 3 C's. What are the

3 C's? Concentration is the first of the three. When a pitcher has lost his confidence, he must go through a process to get it back.

By concentrating better during his routines, he will start to develop the second C called consistency. Consistency is very important to the livelihood of a successful pitcher. Once the first two C's are in place, the one he's lost will be back, and that is confidence. The confidence will be the last of the three but cannot be reached unless the other two are in place. Concentration leads to consistency, and consistency leads to confidence.

What is it that the pitcher needs to concentrate on? They can concentrate on the pre-game throwing program. In professional baseball, it's called the flat ground throwing program. Focus on making those great-located pitches. How many did I locate precisely without having the glove move? Every pitch we need to make in a game are to be done precisely the same during this time. I need a 2-0 secondary pitch in a game for a strike; well this is where we perfect that pitch and count. A pitcher should always be in the game like mode when practicing. We are always rehearsing for the show and working from both the wind-up and the stretch. Concentrate!!!

The bullpens sessions are to be with the mentality that a pitcher will hit every spot that the catcher puts up. Every fastball, curveball, slider, or change-up are to be exactly where you are intending to throw it, by hitting that target. If it's the outside corner, then hit it. If it is to be in the dirt in front of the plate, then bounce the pitch. Concentrate!!!

Whatever facet you're working on, the pitcher will notice how consistent he's becoming and that slowly breeds confidence. This will transition into his performances because he went back to basics. He worked from the ground up. There could be mechanical issues or bad pitch selection, but a pitcher who is in this low point can apply this system to get him back on track.

The successful pitcher has his mind free of any external thoughts that prevent him from making quality pitches. He uses his hand-eye coordination with laser-like precision. He's always in attack mode. If he gets into any trouble, he scans the situation, goes over which pitches will get him the desired result, and then he goes to work and executes. This pitcher is in the complete opposite spectrum from the pitcher who lacks confidence.

The 3 C's is a great way to get any pitcher back on track. With detailed work on these areas the pitcher benefits from utilizing basic sports psychology to his preparation which will reward him during his performances.

CHAPTER 34

Strength and Conditioning In Collaboration with Bruce Peditto

Hard work doesn't guarantee you anything, but without it, you don't stand a chance!

There are only 750 players on this planet playing Major League Baseball. What is one willing to endure and master to set themselves apart from other players who are also trying to be in that selected group? The commitment one has to his craft usually one gets back and then some. What one puts in, one shall get back. How badly does one want it? These are just a few of the terms associated when it comes to paying the price to be successful.

When I played professional baseball in the 80s and early 90s, there was a philosophy the industry followed when it came to strength and conditioning. The pitching coach monitored the running program, which consisted of mainly long- distance running. You would have a choice to run 15 to 20 continues poles or just run outside the stadium for 30 or more minutes if you were the previous game starter or a relief pitcher that went three innings or more. Sprints were also mixed, for about 50 to 60 yards of the distance of 8 to 10 repetitions. On occasions, the pitching coach would throw what we called football passes with the baseball to all the pitchers except the previous days starting pitcher. The football passes would simulate a receiver's running route in football. Starting at one of the foul lines, each pitcher has a baseball in his glove; the pitching coach would stand in centerfield. The pitchers would jog one at a time towards the pitching coach, and as you approached him, one would flip him the ball, and then take off in a sprint to receive the pass the coach was throwing, catching it, and jog to other foul line and start again. It was fun to run on those days because of the comradery the pitchers and pitching coach build with each other. It bonded the group taking your mind off running and focused on catching the ball and not do something goofy that your teammates would get on you for. Even the Dominican and Venezuelan players who didn't know anything about American style football enjoyed this running day.

In those days the commitment to conditioning was solely on the shoulders of each pitcher. If a pitcher lacked commitment, he was left behind as it would trickle into his game and his numbers and performances would take a hit for the worse, and it was a matter of time before they would be sent packing looking for another type of job. In 1987 the organization I was in had one pitching coordinator, and that was it. He visited each affiliate for five days and then moved on to the next city. We would see him around three times a year, which, totaled 15 days for the whole season. If pitchers weren't self-motivated individuals, they would get eaten and spat out of the games.

I was raised in the South Bronx in New York City, and boxing was a big sport for the inner-city kids. It seemed like every neighborhood had a boxing gym around the corner. I attended an after-school program by the name of United Bronx Parents and learned boxing techniques from a boxing coach, which ultimately help me in many self-defense situations in my real life.

I would go to the Golden Gloves every year at Madison Square Garden to watch the finals. Why am I mentioning this? Well, boxing requires lots of running for conditioning in the ring. The better-conditioned an athlete is, the stronger he is mentally. Hard work and dedication to your craft makes an athlete dig deep to go that extra mile when the average human being wants to give up. I adopted this approach in my conditioning.

I started to associate boxing with baseball when it came to conditioning. Boxers go 3-minute rounds and pitchers go three outs per inning. Boxer's fight for 12 rounds and pitchers can go nine innings. In my mind, every inning was like a round, so I had to be in the best shape of my life if I wanted to go nine innings. A boxer has his cornermen, cut man, a trainer who's his coach, and a bucket guy. A pitcher has his teammates on the field defending for him. The boxer and the pitcher are the only ones that face the competition directly, and both are the only ones that go home with the win or the loss. Every hitter was a battle, and I had to win most of those battles if I was to win the war, which was the game.

In 1992 when I played for the Cubs triple-A, in Des Moines, Iowa, I saw the first strength conditioning coach. The strength conditioning coach was roving around the organization, and as he visited the affiliates cities, he started to implement a new running program. It was hard adjusting to the new system at first, being used to doing your running program to get ready for games and maintain your conditioning.

As veteran pitchers, we now had to get used to a strength condition coach telling us what to do and how to do it. The strength coach had a stopwatch, and we needed to do the entire running program under a certain amount of time. We were uncomfortable at first, but with time we started to become used to this new system. This new system set the stage for what would eventually lead to what strength and conditioning are in baseball today. Strength and conditioning coaches are everywhere from the lower youth levels up to the big leagues. And that is the case with almost every athlete now, regardless of sport. The scientific studies on athletes have been booming, and therefore continually changing the way we train.

In the early years of the strength and conditioning coaches in professional baseball, things were much different than what we see today. The concept was new, the science was new, and with most new things, it was far from being perfect. When it came to the strength and conditioning, it was more based on the conditioning, and the strength was not always the focus. The programs were raw and very "one-size-fits-all" which is never good when it comes to training for sports. The end goal of the training must always be reflected in training itself, which was not always the case early on.

In some cases, the programs even went overboard, like when I was with an organization that looked like the players were competing for an Olympic event and there was a wall of fame for the best times in each different categories of competition. Only one player of the best performers reached the major leagues. Some of the players were getting hurt during these events, before ever stepping foot on the playing field.

Since those early years, strength and conditioning programs have evolved and shifted drastically to become more baseball-specific, as well as the ability to be tailored specifically to each position and player as an individual. It was a direction taken as a new type of injuries started to appear, and the science gave new insight for the industry to make some changes in the way they went about training these athletes.

The driving factors behind why strength and conditioning are designed the way that we see today and the reason why it has become such a crucial aspect of the game are twofold. The more commonly coveted focus of the two is the sports performance side. Athletes have been driven by the "bigger, stronger, faster" idea since its conception. With all the new science and research on how to help make athletes more elite, the draw to train has also grown. The more overlooked, but most often the central focus of the training, is injury prevention. If you speak to almost any physical therapist, athletic trainer, or strength and conditioning coach they will most likely tell you that a solid training program will help reduce the risk of injury.

The desire to improve sports performance through strength and conditioning is directly related to the level of competition. Around the world at all levels, in all sports, competition is at an all-time high. Athletes are genetically superior to generations past, and it is leading to the elite levels of play becoming even more cutthroat than ever. In baseball, another significant factor to the rapid rise in competition is due to the international players invading the Major Leagues. It is not only from the Caribbean countries, but Japan, Canada, European countries, and Australia to mention a few. The World Baseball Classic has played a significant role in bringing attention to the global market creating interest throughout the planet. More than ever before does a player needs to be in optimum shape to compete.

When it comes to training programs, whether it be on or off the field, we should keep our health at the forefront. We always need to understand what our body needs given our biological age and our level of play. That is why we must be smart when starting a weight training program. The basis of any resistance training program should be injury prevention as the primary goal, followed by sports performance as it is especially true in a sport like baseball, and even more so when it comes to pitching. What we call "overuse" injuries are prevalent in our sport and our position and can make or break a career. When we look back at the pitchers of the early years, injuries weren't as prevalent as they are today, and weight training wasn't part of their programs. That is counterintuitive to what science and research have shown today. Weights, as we know them today, were almost a taboo in those days.

With all that said, how can we train to accomplish both improve sports performance as well as injury prevention? With a proper balance of resistance training, mobility, and flexibility exercises. Understanding how the body adapts to training and not trying to rush the process is very important. Like with pitch counts and rest days, it is equally important to balance your work to rest ration with strength and conditioning. Following these concepts and working with a strength and conditioning professional can help take your game to the next level while helping ensure that you stay on the field.

In this section, I will provide a strength and conditioning program you can use as a pitcher or as a coach to condition your pitchers. There are two samples of conditioning programs, one for starters and relievers. These samples are based on the conditioning process in season for a young, newly conditioned pitcher. There are also two strength training programs provided as well. The strength programs are broken down into starters and relievers as well. The strength program is created for a pitcher who has been resistance training for at least two times per week for over a year. These programs are just recommendations that can help you if you're starting to build your own. While there are standard exercises and routines that we suggest, each program should be tailored to your needs.

We recommend that you become a student of strength and conditioning because when we are alone, and a coach isn't around us, we need to understand what we are doing as well as why you are doing it. It is always recommended to have supervision when training from an experienced professional. Until you and the professional trainer agree that you are comfortable to train without supervision, it is best to avoid training alone. We must get deeply engaged in maximizing the benefits of every exercise and doing it with the proper technique. Muscle fatigue can lead to injuries, and it is essential to listen to your body to avoid putting yourself in harm's way. The idea is to stay healthy and be on the field performing, not on the sidelines spectating.

It all goes back to am I a self-motivated person and know that I am the toughest competitor the opposition is going to face. Hard work makes us find out about ourselves, and the threshold we are willing to go through to succeed. The rewards will show its face during do or die game situations, in the clutch when our team most needs it. When everything around us is at a fever pitch or heightened level and players around us are nervous and do not want the ball, but we are cool calm and collected to be able to execute and get the job done.

Starter Conditioning Program – In Season

Sample Conditioning Program - In Season

Day of Rotation	Day 1	Day 2	Day 3	Day 4	Day 5
Activity	Start Day	Day after Start	Bullpen Day	Long Toss	Day Before Toss
Focus (Intensity)	Low Impact ("Flush")	Low Intensity	Low - Moderate Intensity	Moderate High Intensity	High Intensity- Sprint
Volume	Low Volume	High Volume	Moderate Volume	Moderate Volume	Low Volume

Reliever Conditioning Program - In Season

Monday	Tuesday	Wednesday	Thursday	Friday	Saturday	Sunday
Sprints	Short Intervals	Long Intervals	Agility	Short Intervals	Long Intervals	OFF

Sample Starter Conditioning Program - In Season

Total Volume for Week - 4300 yards

Day of Rotation	Day 1	Day 2	Day 3	Day 4	Day 5
Day 1	Start Day	Low Impact ("Flush")	Bike or Elliptical	10 mins	
Day 2	Day after Start	Low Intensity/ High Volume	Poles	10 reps	2000 yds
Day 3	Bullpen Day	Low - Moderate intensity / Moderate Volume	3/4 Poles	8 reps	1200 yds
Day 4	Long Toss	Moderate - Hight intensity / Moderate Volume	Full Gassers (Cone at 50 yards)	4 reps	800 yds
Day 5	Day Before Start	High Intensity - Sprint/ Low Volume	30yd Sprints	10 reps	300 yds

Sample Reliever Conditioning Program - In Season

Total Volume for Week - 4700 yards

	Monday	Tuesday	Wednesday	Thursday	Friday	Saturday	Sunday
Type	Sprints	Short Intervals	Long Intervals	Agility	Short Intervals	Long Intervals	OFF
Exercise	30 yd Sprints	1/2 Poles	Poles	Box Drill	60 Yd Sprints	Full Gassers	OFF
Reps	10	8	10	5 Ea.	10	4	OFF
Volume	300	800	2000	200	600	800	OFF

Conditioning Breakdown

- Terminology
  - Volume – sets x reps (for running: distance)
  - Intensity – work level during exercise (how hard/exerting)
  - Intervals – work: rest ratios (10 seconds of work:20 seconds of rest)

Weekly Strength Program

Starter Strength Training

Day of Rotation	Day 1	Day 2	Day 3	Day 4	Day 5
Activity	Start Day	Day after Start	Bullpen Day	Long Toss	Day after Start
Focus	Upper Body /Shoulder Care	Lower Body	Upper Body	Lower Body	OFF

Day of Rotation	Day 1	Day 2	Day 3	Day 4	Day 5
Activity	Start Day	Day after Start	Bullpen Day	Long Toss	Day before Start
Focus	Shoulder Care	Total Body	Shoulder Care	Total Body	OFF

Reliever Strength Training

Monday	Tuesday	Wednesday	Thursday	Friday	Saturday	Sunday
Upper Body	OFF	Lower Body	OFF	Total Body	OFF	OFF

Sample Strength Training

Upper Body	
Exercise	Sets x Reps
MB Chest Pass	2 x 10
Reverse Crunch	2 x 10
DB Row	3 x 10
DB Bench Press	3 x 10
Lat Pull-down	3 x 10
Band Pull Apart	2 x 10
Open Books	2 x 10 each side
Triceps Extension	2 x 10

Lower Body

Scissor Jumps	2 x 8 each side
Dead Bugs	2 x 10
Squat (Body Weight or Goblet)	3 x 10
Kneeling Hip Adductor Stretch	3 x 10 sec each side
Single Leg Glute Bridge	3 x 10 each side
Pigeon Stretch	3 x 10 sec each side
Side Lunges	2 x 10 each side
Stability Ball Hamstring Curl	2 x 10

Total Body #1

2 x 8 each side	2 x 8 each side
Push Ups	2 x 6-10
KB Dead lift	2 x 10
BB Row	2 x 10
Reverse Lunge	3 x 10 each side
Farmers Carry	2 x 15 yds
Plank	2 x 30 sec

Total Body #2	
Exercise	**Sets x Reps**
Squat Jump	**2 x 5**
Standing Cable Row	**2 x 10**
Incline DB Bench Press	**2 x 10**
Single Leg RDL	**2 x 10 each side**
Monster Walks	**2 x 15 yds**
Pallof Press	**2 x 10 each side**

The shoulder is the joint that has the most range of motion in the body and because of this large range of motion, it can lead to shoulder joint problems especially for pitchers. The shoulder is made up of bones, joints, ligaments, tendons, muscles, nerves, blood vessels, and bursae sac. As pitchers, we need to take the time to become aware and learn about the nature of the shoulder. The intricacies of how it functions, how it can be injured, and the road to recovery and return after an injury are the foundation to the longevity and health of your shoulder. While the injuries can be inevitable in some, very rare instances, they are most often preventable with proper arm care and consciousness when it comes to pitching mechanics and frequency. When pitchers have a shoulder injury, it is a long, difficult recovery and rehabilitation process.

The levers method has addressed the issues that put the elbow and shoulder in a compromising position, which can make a pitcher more susceptible to injury. We discussed that pitchers who lead with lower half, precisely with the hips and stay in the backward C longer down the slope with good shoulder and belt line going against the gravity, creating more energy are at dramatically less risk of getting injured. With the implementation of a proper arm care program, we can reduce that risk of injury even more.

Caring for our arms is as important if not more important than anything else we do in this game. With the amount of throwing a pitcher does during a season one has to have an excellent arm exercise program to maintain and keep you healthy throughout your campaign. It is much better to be a participant as appose to a spectator on the sidelines watching your teammates perform on the field.

When it comes to implementing an arm care program, there are a few things we want to consider from the start. First and foremost is that we recommend consulting a professional to help introduce and familiarize you with the program during the initial phases. In this situation, a professional would be a strength and conditioning coach, an athletic trainer, or a physical therapist. The second focus you want to keep in mind is that these exercises are chosen to help care for the shoulder by moving the scapula, or shoulder blade, through specific patterns. These specific patterns help train and strengthen the muscles that stabilize the shoulder throughout the range of motion we move through while pitching. The reason we put a focus on the movement patterns and why they are chosen is very important. These exercises require very little resistance or weight to provide a great benefit. When performing these exercises, it is not necessary to load weight as you do for the other exercises in your normal weight training program. The focus should always be on using the proper muscles and paths to move through the range of motion. That is why we recommend working with a professional to help start the program.

Resistance bands and very light (two to three pounds) dumbbells are two key ways to strengthen the rotator cuff. The resistance bands can also be used to warm up and get the arm loose before a pitcher starts throwing and getting ready to pitch in a game. We will go over a group of exercises that can be performed to help protect and keep your rotator cuff healthy and strong.

Exercise 1 – Front Raise

- The exercise will be done at a 45-degree angle in front of your body, not directly in front of your shoulder and not directly out to the side of your body
- You will have your thumbs up hand basically in a fist
- Raise up to shoulder height, not any higher

- Concentrate on that front part of the shoulder, isolating the rotator cuff
- Raise hands up quickly and come down slow around 3 seconds or so

Exercise 2 – Lateral Raise.

- Palms facing down
- Arms go out to the side, in line with your body
- Lift is even with your shoulders (Body and arms resembles the letter T when looking in the mirror)
- Raise hands up and come down slow around 3 seconds or so

Exercise 3 – Inverted (reverse) Hand Raise

- Same starting position as Exercise 1
- Have your pinkies facing up to the ceiling and thumbs down
- Raise arms to shoulder height not above

Exercise 4 – External Rotation

- Laying on your side if using no resistance or a dumbbell; If using resistance bands stand sideways with the active arm on the outside
- Roll a small towel and place it between your upper arm and rib cage, just above the elbow
- Bent on the elbow to 90 degrees with your forearm pointing forward
- Externally rotate (outwards) as far as is comfortable, do not force it past your natural range of motion

Exercise 5 – Internal Rotation

- Laying on your back if using no resistance or a dumbbell; If using resistance bands stand sideways with the active arm on the inside

- Roll a small towel and place it between your upper arm and rib cage, just above the elbow
- Bent on the elbow to 90 degrees with your forearm pointing forward
- Internally rotate (inwards) as far as is comfortable, making sure to keep the towel tight between your arm and rib cage

Additional Direction:

1. These exercises should be performed 3 to 4 times per week or every other day
2. Exercises should be performed in sets of 10 repetitions for three sets
3. Be sure to perform the exercises with proper posture in mind, keeping the shoulder blades retracted
4. If you do not have a towel available, you can use a baseball, or your opposite hand made into a fist
5. Be sure to select the proper resistance; the focus is on proper form not how much weight
6. This is not about how quickly I can do the reps; it's about technique and doing them at a steady, controlled pace

After reading all the guidelines and recommendations for strength and conditioning provided here, it is important to remember what the main goal is. When it comes to training to become a better pitcher you need to have a program with that as the end goal. Your focus should not be to lift a specific amount of weight or to look like a bodybuilder at the end of your program. As with pitching in a game, you must be diligent and take each pitch and each workout one at a time while knowing they are the building blocks to help you reach your end goal.

About the Author

Hector Berrios is a professional baseball pitching coach with over 30 years of experience as a pitcher and a coach. He has worked with five different organizations and has been part of the development process of hundreds of pitchers who have gone on to pitch in the Major Leagues. As a pitcher, he reached the Triple-A level with three different organizations, and as a coach, he worked with some of the best pitching minds the game has to offer. His pitching staff have found their way to being at the top of most of the leagues in ERA and least number of walks. As a student of the game, he's infused the best routines, results, and techniques to blend them into a unique system that has worked for the youth league, high school, college, and Major League pitchers. His passion for teaching has transcended to many parts of the world as an ambassador for baseball, working with coaches and pitchers from Taiwan, Austria, Mexico, Venezuela, Puerto Rico, and the Dominican Republic.

Testimonials

Ronald Bolaños, right-handed pitcher San Diego Padres

"Meeting Hector Berrios was a life-changing experience that transformed me from a position player in Cuba to a Major League pitcher in September of 2019 with an increased velocity of 99/100 mph. Hector taught me everything about pitching from A to Z and I learned so much in such a short period of time. He worked on my mechanics which caused my fastball to jump from 88 - 91 mph to 93 to 96 mph during my first showcase, eventually touching 97mph. The spin on my curveball improved and my change-up became very deceptive. After working out during the mornings he would have lesson plans in the evenings to teach me how to develop bullpen routines, in game situations, pitch selections, how to set up hitters by establishing command of my pitches, and how to expand to put away hitters. We worked diligently on controlling runners on first and second base to prevent unnecessary runs from scoring. Once I started to develop in all these areas, I signed a multimillion-dollar contract with the San Diego Padres. After each of my professional seasons, I continued to work with Hector to enhance everything I learned. He has been a teacher, a mentor, a friend, and a father figure who made my transition stateside an easy one. The passion he has for pitching and teaching is a true gift."

Vladimir Gutierrez, right-handed pitcher Cincinnati Reds

"My fortunes completely changed when I started working with Hector and it wasn't long before I landed a multimillion-dollar contract with the Cincinnati Reds. My experience in the United States did not get off to a good start. I was awarded the rookie of the year in the Cuban professional league and was ready to take my talents to the next level. Once I arrived in the United States I got to work and was ready for my first showcase in which all MLB teams came to watch me pitch. It was a very disappointing experience as my mechanics were off and my velocity was down.

I did not receive any contract offers and there was no interest from any of the clubs. However, I started working with Hector and he showed me how my mechanics were not synchronized or leveraged which resulted in a lack of command and velocity. We did lots of sensory drills, which immediately drove my velocity from 91 mph to a high of 98 mph. He helped me to establish good solid routines which enhanced every facet of my pitching. Hector taught me how to pitch by breaking down strategies, pitch-selection, and controlling runners at first and second base. I think back on the vital role Hector played in my life as he helped shape my destiny and baseball career. I work with Hector every offseason to continue to improve my abilities to gain an edge on the competition."

Pedro Beato, right-handed pitcher Philadelphia Phillies

"After working with Hector Berrios and applying the stuff in *Unleash the Pitcher in You*, I got back to the big leagues and saved 67 games at the AAA level (32 and 35) on back to back years. Back in 2014, I was up in the big leagues with the Atlanta Braves. I relied more on my secondary stuff to pitch because I couldn't use my fastball effectively. Hector taught me how to become more efficient and I was better able to work my fastball. My direction to the plate and explosion of the lower half were two key factors for my success. I recommend *Unleash the Pitcher in You* to anyone who wants to take their pitching skills to the next level."

Ray Burris, former Major League pitcher

"I have worked with Hector Berrios for the last four years and have seen his work up close and personal. His attention to detail is second to none and as a result, has touched the lives of so many aspiring pitchers to reach levels beyond their expectations. His teaching is very contagious and fun. *Unleash the Pitcher in You* is a perfect illustration of how to develop a pitcher with all the inner the secrets he shares."

Jordan Hershiser, right-handed pitcher—Los Angeles Dodgers Organization

"I started working with Hector Berrios at the end of spring training in 2014. Before working with Hector, I was having a lot of difficulties repeating my delivery and getting the most of my body. I remember the first thing Hector noticed when watching me play catch was that I was throwing the ball like an infielder, not a pitcher. I was cutting off my arm path and not releasing the ball out front. We immediately began working on getting my arm and entire body behind and through the baseball. We spent the time that day throwing and emphasizing the correct finish and I could immediately see results in how the ball came out of my hand. I was disappointed to not make a roster out of spring training, but it turned out to be a huge blessing in disguise. In extended spring training, a place for most first-year professionals, there I was, a 25-year-old who was on the last legs of a minor league career. Hector talked to me and told me that he thought I had a lot more in the tank. He looked at my tall 6'7" fame and realized that I was not using my body effectively and efficiently to deliver the baseball. The first thing we focused on in extended spring training was my head position when I was in my set position. Hector noticed that I was leading or "leaking" with my head when I was going down the hill and he had me come set with my head over the ball of my back foot to keep it there until I finished my leg kick. This helped me use my leverage in the correct sequence and helped me use my lower half to drive myself down the mound. Once I began to get comfortable with the changes we were making, I was able to increase my velocity from 87-88 miles per hour to 90-93 miles per hour. This jump in velocity greatly helped my pitching career, and I was able to pitch off of my fastball more than I had before I worked with Hector. Every day at 6:30 am Hector would be out on the practice mounds waiting for any pitcher in extended spring who wanted to get some early work done. Those morning sessions on the mound followed meetings where we discussed the art of pitching and different game strategies were some of the most beneficial work I have done during my baseball life. The enthusiasm he had for pitching and coaching was infectious and it made practice enjoyable. Of course, having results also helped the enjoyment factor, and I started seeing great improvements in my velocity and command of my pitches because of the things I changed while working with Hector. We continued to work daily on ironing out the changes that we needed to make, and once I had one part down pat, we would begin to touch on another aspect that would improve my delivery. The different drills that I did with Hector, including mirror work, dry work, dry work off of the back slope of the mound, and bullpens all helped to reinforce the changes that we were trying to make. Hector did a very good job of accurately explaining the reasons behind his coaching and never once did I think what he was teaching was outdated or out of touch with reality. Soon enough I was beginning to have great success in the extended games and was very pleased with how I was throwing the ball and how my arm was recovering in between appearances. Since I was using my lower half and my levers more effectively, I was able to throw the ball with less strain on my arm. I have had two major arm surgeries, both while I was in college, and since then, I had developed some negative habits to protect my arm, but what I was doing was putting added stress on my arm. The work that we did with Hector off the field also had a great impact on my career. Our morning meetings consisted of different topics relating to pitching, and the message was always clear and direct. Hector had gathered different videos of major league pitchers to help demonstrate some of the fundamental steps in delivering the baseball that almost every major league pitcher does. Hector also used PowerPoints to display different statistics relating to pitching such as the percentage of strikes thrown and the batting average of a hitter in different ball-strike counts. These meetings helped reinforce what we were seeing in our games and I could easily see how the information Hector was presenting to us was tangible and applicable to our careers. Hector had a great attitude every day and it became contagious to the guys around him. He was always ready to help and seemed to truly enjoy the success of others. All the work that Hector did with myself and all the other pitchers in extended spring was extremely beneficial, and I still go back to things I have learned from him while I'm working on fixing something by myself. Soon enough I was called to head to Midland, Michigan to pitch for the Dodgers A-ball affiliate the Great Lakes Loons. I was able to continue the success and feeling I had of working with Hector for the rest of the season and I ended up having a pretty successful year for the Loons. I continued to practice the lessons and drills I learned with Hector during the season, and whenever I felt like I had a bad outing I would go back to what we talked about in Arizona and it seemed to set me straight. It was no surprise to me that multiple pitchers who worked with Hector at that time ended up having very successful years after extended spring was over and I look forward to continuing to work with Hector in the future. Overall, I really enjoyed my time working with him and I truly appreciate everything he has done for me, not only as a baseball player but also as a human being."

Brant Whiting, catcher Los Angeles Dodgers Organization

"Coming into my first professional season, I had never been given a chance to call my own game behind the plate. At Stanford, our pitching coach called all the pitches and never really explained his philosophy to the catchers or the pitchers. Stanford is no different than most college programs, where catchers just blindly look at the pitch signs and then relay them to the pitcher without analyzing the batter or game situation. Because of this methodology, most college catchers' pitch-calling skills are lacking, at best.

I started off the professional season calling pitches without a purpose. I had a vague understanding of the theory of effective velocity, which suggests the perceived velocity of pitch changes based on the location of the pitch. A fastball inside appears faster to a hitter than a fastball away because they need to react sooner in order to put the ball in play. However, I didn't really know how to put this into practice. Additionally, I never thought about how the situation in a game might affect how to call pitches to a batter. In certain situations, a 3-1 off-speed pitch may be acceptable, whereas in others it is an absolute no-no. My first, couple of games, were very frustrating as my pitch calling was questioned frequently. I remember calling a 3-1 changeup to "fool" or "trick" a batter in a game where we were winning by 1 run late in the game. Hector really got on me from the dugout because the call resulted in a walk. I thought it was a good call. The hitter had been on the fastball all day so I thought he would be fooled by a changeup and would roll over or swing through it. Another situation, I remember distinctly, was against the Cubs when there were runners on 1st and 2nd with 2 outs. The game was tied in the bottom of the ninth. Like the above situation, the hitter had been on the fastball all game (he hit a homerun the at bat before on a fastball). This at bat, he took a couple of good swings at the slider. So, on a 2-2 count, I called a changeup which was the pitcher's third best command pitch. The batter hit a double in the gap to win the game.

It's clear from the above situations that coming into pro ball, I called pitches with the attempt to outsmart the batter. As I learned very quickly, this type of pitch calling often led to game-winning hits, or momentum-changing runs. I finally hit my breaking point and asked Hector for a meeting to go over my pitch calling and the dos and don'ts of calling a game. This is where I learned that pitch calling is more of a reaction to the previous pitch rather than trying to think 2 or 3 pitches ahead. You can have an idea of how you want to approach a batter, but if he does something to change that idea mid at bat, you must react. If the batter is late on the fastball, don't just go to changeup because that was your plan; throw another fastball until he shows that he is on that pitch. Then go to something off-speed to catch him leaning. Use your eyes to call pitches, not what you think might trick the batter. The batter will tell you what you should throw next if you are paying attention to his reaction to the previous pitch.

The game plan that Hector devised and pounded into our heads in the pitcher/catcher meetings proved to be very effective when properly applied in the game. To apply it, you must trust what you see. Start the batter with a fastball away. If he takes a pitch, repeat that pitch. If he is late on the fastball, throw it again. If he is early, throw an off-speed pitch. If he looks terrible on a curveball, throw the curveball again. This is all built off of the first pitch, and you can never go wrong starting with a low and away fastball. That is the pitcher's money pitch. When in doubt, go with the pitcher's money pitch. The down and away fastball is not a pitch that the typical batter can do damage with. A good hitter will often take a 2-0 outside fastball because their sights are set on the inner half of the plate.

As I applied this game plan in the games, I began to have greater success in my pitch calling. I slowly learned through experience the keys to look for in a batter to determine how he is reacting to a pitch. One of the most important things that I learned is how to put a batter into "swing mode" as Hector called it. If you pound the strike zone, the batter becomes uncomfortable as the count becomes more unfavorable to him. As he becomes more uncomfortable, he becomes more defensive and will swing more readily at pitches that are not in the zone. A common sequence that might put a batter into swing mode is as follows: start with a fastball low and away for a strike. If the batter swings and is late, he will adjust his timing for the next pitch. Call fastball away again and he is on the pitch but fouls it straight back. Now the batter is in a 2-strike count and is very vulnerable. If the pitcher can throw a slider in the dirt that starts on the same plane as the previous fastballs, the batter is very likely to swing through it for strike 3. Putting the batter into this defensive, swing-happy mode is one of the major goals in pitch calling.

The final lesson I learned was how to use effective velocity to keep the batter off-balance. As I have already mentioned, the location of a pitch will determine the perceived velocity of that pitch. An inside fastball can be perceived up to 5 miles per hour faster than a fastball down the middle, and an outside fastball will be perceived up to 5 miles per hour slower than a fastball down the middle. Using this theory, you could effectively pitch just using the fastball. However, when you throw off-speed pitches in the repertoire, you can really throw a batter off balance. Hector would get on me about this often, as there were many times where my pitch calling helped the batter's odds because of the theory of perceived velocity.

220

For example, I may have called a fastball away after a change-up inside. Those two pitches in those locations would be perceived at the same velocity, and therefore the batter would react like it was the same type of pitch.

As I began to get more games under my belt, the theory of effective velocity started to click. After a long summer, I was finally able to put all of Hector's teachings together in my final game which ended up being a no-hitter. This result is the culmination of a summer's worth of hard work, great teaching, and trust in the application of the game plan and theory of effective velocity. Thanks to Hector's coaching and his effective game plan, I really understood the tenets of calling a good game. I am by no means perfect at this point, but I now have a great foundation to build from. I will continue to use Hector's game plan and theories as I move up in the organization only changing when the hitter's reaction demands it. Trust what you see, not what you think. Your eyes will tell you what pitch should be called."

Will Hibbs, RHP – 2016 Philadelphia Phillies Organization

"My first professional outing was in Lowell, Massachusetts near the beginning of Short Season A ball for the Philadelphia Phillies organization. I was a recent "senior sign" in the 19th round, so I felt I needed to hit the ground running and excel from day one. I was brought into the game in the 8th inning with runners on first and second base and no outs (Thanks, Skip!). A sacrifice bunt and a 17 hopper, seeing-eye-single later, I had my first blown save and the first loss of my professional career; not a great start for someone who was already putting a lot of pressure on himself. But hey, at least I got the first one out of the way. That first outing sticks in my head because it reminds me of where I started, how much I had to learn, and how differently I view certain aspects of pitching now. The best thing I did for myself in my first season was to focus on learning something every day: learning a new grip for a pitch, focusing on my mechanics and learning how to better use my lower half in my delivery, learning how to travel on those eight hour bus trips to Vermont (and still be ready to pitch in the first game off the bus), learning how to better communicate in Spanish, etc. Hector Berrios played a pivotal role in this process. He showed me I needed to stay open-minded in my environment, to allow myself to grow as a pitcher and a person. Minor League baseball is a lifestyle shock, no doubt about it, but I commend the Phillies organization and all the respective coaches on handling the process the right way. Whether it was pitching, strength and conditioning, nutrition, personal life, or Sunday Chapel, it was managed with purposeful intent and focused direction. This past season (2016) was one of the most enjoyable times I've had as a pitcher. It was extremely rewarding to see my improvements in the game after working countless hours with Hector daily(seriously...... every. single. day.). This training wasn't limited to pitching mechanics alone; we addressed the mental side of the game daily as well. Prior to each game, the pitching staff met to review the previous game, strategize for the game that day, and focus on our key concepts. Hector reminded us of the importance of holding runners: differentiating between one and four second looks to keep the runner off balance, and utilizing a "half-way" look with a runner on second base in order to effectively see him out of our peripheral vision (while giving the appearance that the pitcher isn't paying attention to the runner). Utilizing these tools and strategies almost instantly slowed the game down for our pitchers, allowing us to efficiently make quality pitches while shutting down the opponent's running game. Our other key concept was pitch command and delivery. The goal is to make every pitch look the same out of the pitcher's hand, releasing it "through the tunnel". Making sure the release point is the same, regardless of the type of pitch thrown, forces the batter to respect every pitch in your arsenal and makes it impossible for him to eliminate a certain pitch based on a different release point than the pitcher's other offerings. Once you can do this consistently, the game really opens up. Quality low and away fastballs (creating a bad bat angle for the batter, usually resulting in weak contact or foul balls), shaving the black of home plate on the inside corner (creating a higher perceived velocity to the batter), and breaking balls in the dirt when ahead in the count (ideally causing a swing and miss) are keys to success for pitchers. These tools, properly utilized via pitches delivered from the same location (through the tunnel), make it easier to disrupt the batter's timing and enhancing the pitcher's success. From hip torque to mounting the back leg, dumping the hands to initiating that ever-powerful "backward C", creating the opposing angles with the hip and shoulder line, and driving off of the back leg while the arm explodes through the "tunnel", I was able to see rapid improvements. Hector and I began to see my velocity tick up a few miles per hour, my breaking pitches tighten up, and (most importantly) a significant enhancement in my consistency. All of this was due to the constant "dry work" in between outings. I clearly recall each modification we made; Hector working with me to instill these tools into my mind and my mechanics, while making sure I maintained a "laser-like" focus on every pitch. This ideology of pitching transfers quickly and effectively from training to the mound in game situations and is sure to assist any aspiring pitcher to elevate and polish his game."--

Brian Bowles, right-handed pitcher Toronto Blue Jays 2001-2003

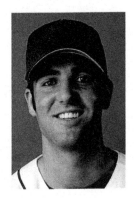

"I had a 7.50 ERA and was on the brink of being released by the Toronto Blue Jays until I had the good fortune of having Hector Berrios as my pitching coach. A year and a half later, I was in the big leagues with Toronto and I could not have done it without Hector. He has a deep understanding of the pitching delivery and how to maximize a pitcher's velocity. His knowledge of all facets of pitching, from pitch sequencing to the running game is why *Unleash the Pitcher in You* is a must read for any pitcher who is serious about maximizing their potential.

Jose De León, right-handed pitcher Cincinnati Reds

"I've never met anyone as passionate as Héctor when it comes to pitching. His teaching is precise, direct, and aggressive, yet smooth: so, will be your pitching after reading *Unleash the Pitcher in You*. He takes pitching to a whole different level, which is why *Unleash the Pitcher in You* is simply a must-read for every young pitcher, parent, coach or just anyone who wants to elevate their game on the art of pitching."

Notes

1. "Library of Congress." Carl Reid. A study on injured pitchers from the 1950s to 2004 pg.19

2. Zimniuch, Fran. "2010. Fireman: The Evolution of the Closer in Baseball" pg.19

3. Chaves, Rafael. Levers Method-Pitching Delivery Checkpoints. MILB Pitching Coordinator (Checkpoints used in the Minor league Pitching Manuel) pg.32

4. Natal, Bob. Methods to Prevent Stealing Signs From 2nd Base. MILB Catching Coordinator, pg.134

5. Peterson, Rick. Peak Performance Triangle. Peak Performance Triangles are used in Major League Baseball Manuals and PowerPoints pg.138,140

6. Mackenzie, Brian. Components of Fitness, www.brianmac.co.uk/conditon.htm. pg.148

7. Chee, Rosie. "Training Power Systems: Anaerobic and Aerobic Training Methods!" Bodybuilding.com, 18 Jan. 2019, www.bodybuilding.com/fun/anaerobic-aerobic-training-methods.htm. Pg.149

8. Doran, George T. The History and Evolution of SMART Goals | AchieveIt. www.achieveit.com/resources/blog/the-history-and-evolution-of-smart-goals. Pg.152

9. Knapp, Rick. Chart was used in a pitching talk to players pg.162

10. Peterson, Rick. Ahead Early Behind Charting. Used in Major League Baseball Manuals and PowerPoints pg.167

11. "TruMedia - www.tru-media.com. Major League averages by counts pg. 170

Bibliography

Brown, Daniel, and Daniel Brown. "Pitch Counts? Not in Marichal-Spahn Era." The Mercury News, The Mercury News, 1 July 2013, www.mercurynews.com/2013/07/01/pitch-counts-not-in-marichal-spahn-era.

Chee, Rosie. "Training Power Systems: Anaerobic and Aerobic Training Methods!" Bodybuilding.com, Bodybuilding.com, 18 Jan. 2019, www.bodybuilding.com/fun/anaerobic-aerobic-training-methods.htm.

Elsevier. "Home." 1st Edition, Churchill Livingstone, 1 Apr. 2008, www.elsevier.com/books/churchill-livingstones-dictionary-of-sport-and-exercise-science-and-medicine/jennett/978-0-443-10215-8.

Kaplan, Jim. Greatest Game Ever Pitched: Juan Marichal, Warren Spahn, and the Pitching Duel of the Century. Triumph Books, 2013.

Knapp, Rick. Charts used in a pitching talk to players

Library of Congress. Carl Reid. A study on injured pitchers from the 1950s to 2004

Mackenzie, Brian. Components of Fitness, www.brianmac.co.uk/conditon.htm.

Peterson, Rick. Peak Performance Triangle. Peak Performance Triangles are used in Major League Baseball Manuals and PowerPoints
TruMedia - www.tru-media.com/. Major League averages by counts

Zimniuch, Fran. "2010. Fireman: The Evolution of the Closer in Baseball"

Made in the USA
Columbia, SC
25 September 2024

42997037R00128